Felicity Hayward

Does My Butt Look Big in This?

☆ A BODY POSITIVITY MANIFESTO ☆

greenfinch

First published in Great Britain in 2022 by

Greenfinch
An imprint of Quercus Editions Ltd
Carmelite House
50 Victoria Embankment
London EC4Y 0DZ

An Hachette UK company

A CIP catalogue record for this book is available from the British Library

HB ISBN 9781529417333
eBook ISBN 9781529417357

10 9 8 7 6 5 4 3 2 1

Typeset and design by Tokiko Morishima
Illustrations by Burcu Koleli

Printed and bound in China

Picture credits
Pages 6, 27, 42, 66, 114, 131, 139 © Lauren Thom; pages 13, 156, 178 © Tomila Katsman; page 22 © Roderick Deeds Ejuetami; pages 81, 119 © Sylwia Szyplik. All other photos © Felicity Hayward.

This book is dedicated to my best friend Sybil, my beautiful, stylish and kind grandmother who has always taught me to be unapologetically myself, no matter what. I wouldn't be where I am without you.

Author's Note

Hello babes, and welcome to *Does My Butt Look Big in This?* I have written this book from my experience as a curvy woman and I have other women like me in mind. That being said, I hope that, in many places, these pages will resonate with those of you who have had your own different, and potentially more difficult, journeys due to your size, age, race, ability or gender. It goes without saying that, despite the lack of size representation in mainstream media, my position and my privilege as a white, cisgender and able-bodied woman has permitted me access to spaces and opportunities that many are still fighting for. Though there is some change, it's at a glacial speed, so before reading my journey I implore you lovely readers to research, follow and engage with the incredible voices in the body positivity space who are not only fighting for size diversity, but who are also pushing for increased visibility and representation of disabled bodies, people of colour and trans people, to name a few examples. In particular, I want to give a special shout out and thanks to Sabey Dantsira, Kelly Knox, Tinar Dandajena, Mariah Idrissi and Clara Holmes.

Special thanks to my amazing publishing, editing, design and management team for being incredibly supportive, patient and understanding during my first experience writing a book. Anna, Marnie, Nicole, Kerry, Lindsay, Tokiko and Burcu: you are the best, even when I'm sending ideas at 3am in the morning; we did it and I'm so thankful for you all.

This is my journey into the body positive space, and I hope that my honest words and my insights into the fashion industry will open your eyes to the importance of being your true, authentic self.

Felicity x

Contents

Introduction

I'm not sure how old you are, but when I was younger there was always a defining question that would be thrown around before the school disco, while changing for PE or getting ready to go uptown to meet your besties on a Saturday. And that question was, 'Babes, be honest ... does my butt look big in this?'

Now, this is a very open-ended question, which can be answered in so many ways, both positive and negative. All I remember growing up in the 1990s was that the answer would always be, 'No, of course it doesn't look big' (with the subtext being: let's do all we can to hide it).

In this book I want to explore this question, pull apart its meaning and ultimately find an answer to the really big issue that lies behind it: why are we being so unkind to our bodies?

The moment we become poorly, we pray to our bodies to mend us from the inside, but when we are feeling well we battle with our appearance on the outside.

Isn't it bizarre that with everything going on in the world, everything that is constantly thrown at us in life, we still seek to punish ourselves by criticizing the way our bodies look, focusing on the way we assume we appear to other people or negatively comparing our looks to the popular kids in school or to the seemingly 'picture perfect' bodies on social media?

I was never in the popular group in school. I was the one who was queuing up outside Woolworths on my own before school in my Dr Martens, my rucksack covered in patches and pins, listening to my CD Walkman while waiting to buy the latest Incubus album. I was the one who wore clothes from charity shops and got style advice from my nan. But there was still a contentment there when I was younger and I do believe it was because there wasn't any social media to feed my insecurity. I didn't even have a camera phone until I was around 16. We had dial-up internet and a rubbish phone signal, so I would spend my evenings watching old VHS films in my bedroom, playing *Snake* on my Nokia 3310 or making mix CDs for friends.

The only time I would notice any public body shaming back then would be on the covers of gossip magazines where they would be slating someone for being a UK size 14 (US size 10) and wearing a bikini on holiday. Fortunately, most of the time I was in my own little bubble so I didn't even notice this, but that quickly changed when I became a young adult, as social media became more of a point of reference for everything from fashion and beauty to culture and entertainment.

There were hardly any large women on our TV screens back then and, if there were, they would invariably be cast as the 'funny one' – never the love interest, the confident one or the boss. That itself causes a lot of body-image issues when you never see yourself reflected positively onscreen. Things are starting to change these days but there is still a long way to go. And the low self-esteem we experience is going to persist until we can get to a place of understanding that there is more than one way of being beautiful.

I was lucky when I was growing up as I had so much love and encouragement from my nan. I loved finding eccentric fashion at car boot sales; I loved going to concerts, jumping on trains, sneaking on the guest list and flogging spare tickets outside. I've always been a grafter, I've always had so-called 'balls', but I lacked any confidence in my body, hiding myself away for a long time under layers and layers of clothing. If I'm being honest, my vintage secondhand sequin jackets were essentially my armour. I guess deep down I wore them as a big middle finger to the high street, to the times I couldn't buy the same jeans as my friends, to the gossip magazines and to the TV channels that didn't seem to cater for my size or represent my body shape. But despite the outward bravado there was still an insecurity there about my body and I guess my eccentric style was my coping mechanism.

I'm writing this book because I don't want anyone else to go through those moments of anxiety over the vessel that literally keeps your blood pumping, your thoughts processing and your dreams flowing. Your body is your best friend. So in these pages I want to tell you about all the things I've learned about myself and the industry I'm in – and how I've grown to love and feel comfortable in my body.

> ### 'Your body is your best friend.'

Ultimately, this book has been created with my little sister in mind. She has the same body shape as me, as well as developing stretch marks at a younger age – the ones that are bright cherry red and will eventually fade. But she didn't try to wash them off in the shower like I did; she didn't cover up her body from her partner and wear high-waisted knickers because she thought she had ruined her body by simply just growing. Instead she learned to accept them pretty quickly and that's because she had more access to representation, understanding and love.

If you think about it, when a plant grows bigger and produces stronger leaves, when it blooms and flowers in different colours, we find it beautiful and celebrate it. But when changes happen on a human body, ones that haven't been normalized and are therefore not admired or understood, so often that's when the body confidence fades and we try to hide ourselves away. I believe it doesn't have to be that way.

My sister was lucky. There is a big age gap between us and things are changing now. Although she grew up in the social media world where comparison is the thief of joy, she also had me as a real-life body-confident role model cheering her on. I was able to show her that stretch marks, cellulite and body hair were normal. She didn't feel so alienated by society.

I want this book to fill the role of your older sibling, older cousin or best friend. Something you turn to when you want a little boost. When you're in need of a little confidence pick-me-up. It will be there waiting for you to turn the pages, make notes and think deeper.

I'll also be looking into the hype around 'body positivity' – how you can recognize who is harnessing it for good and who is simply using their influence and platform to make money on the back of insecurities that society pushes onto us. I want to explore how we speak to ourselves about our bodies and how that's changed over the previous decades, taking us right up to the present day. I also want to help you to identify the underlying factors that are influencing how you really feel about YOUR figure.

I will be asking the questions, giving you my best answers and providing positive solutions to spring open the padlock on that suitcase of confidence you've been hiding in the attic!

Self-love is very important to me now and I wish there had been some sort of self-love bootcamp when I was younger that could have taught me how to truly appreciate myself and stop comparing myself to others. Then again, if we all loved ourselves, millions of pounds would be lost in sales of products that are marketed to us to supposedly create the 'best versions of ourselves'. But what if we already are the best versions of ourselves and just can't see it?

Let's tackle that self-love, babe, no matter what size your derrière is.

My Journey into Body Positivity

You know what, babes, I haven't always been confident. I preach self-love but that was something that had to be learned and it didn't come overnight.

I remember exactly where I was when I first discovered stretch marks on my body. I was 17 years old and staying at my ex-boyfriend's place in Leeds. It was a brown, brick-terraced house on a badly cobbled street with tons of character – one of those ones that look like they're straight out of a scene in *Peaky Blinders* (if they ever came to Yorkshire).

We had just come back from the pub; I was getting ready for bed and went to take a shower. I was getting undressed and noticed some marks on my belly – you know, the kind of marks you get when you've worn jeans to a three-course pub meal and you can't wait to take them off. The kind that temporarily appear because your waistband doesn't have much stretch and now, after a large pudding, your clothes are screaming to get off your body.

The thing is, I took a shower and those marks didn't seem to fade. I remember wiping the mirror with my towel (I had definitely spent far too long in the shower and now the whole

room was steamed up), feeling confused as to why there were deep cherry marks on my belly that simply didn't wash off.

It took a while for the penny to drop that they were stretch marks. The problem is I had never seen these marks on any of my girlfriends, on any celebrities, actresses or even on my mum. Stretch marks were for pregnant women only, surely? I literally hadn't seen them anywhere online or on screen.

When it hit me that this was the only explanation, I remember the panic, the absolute fear that I had wrecked my body for life. I was devastated. This was my fault; I had ruined myself. My partner was not going to find me attractive any more. I would need to hide these marks with high-waisted knickers and tights and not let him see me naked until I could get rid of them. Imagine that. Imagine thinking you had ruined your body by simply growing?

> **'Imagine thinking you had ruined your body by simply growing?'**

I spent all the money I could on products to try to fix the marks and oils to reduce the redness, which together came to nearly the cost of my food shop for the week. And of course, none of it made any difference.

I wish I could go back and tell my younger self that stretch marks and other such skin changes are a part of growth; our bodies change and this is totally normal. I wish I could have told my younger self that the cherry marks would die down and turn into an electric silver colour, that they would be my

'I now see my stretch marks as my roots that have grown into a tree of life.'

lightning bolts, my tiger stripes, and that they would carry me on my journey to self-discovery.

I wish I could have told myself that high-street retailers would eventually start creating more stylish plus-size collections, that they would start to use actual full-figured models on their websites and that there would be a defining moment when they also would stop editing out stretch marks, cellulite and skin textures. That this change would go across the whole board from the petite sizing to the plus-size range. We would see smaller models with cellulite and stretch marks and we would witness how this would go viral online, helping to normalize all types of bodies.

> **'Nothing is ever truly broken and there is always beauty in the imperfect.'**

I wish I could have told myself that ten years later I would be appearing on a television programme promoting positive body image, painting my and other women's stretch marks with gold paint. That I would be telling the other women that in Japan, when a piece of pottery is broken, they still see its beauty and they repair the item with powdered gold. They believe nothing is ever truly broken and there is always beauty in the imperfect. I wish I had known that by doing this I would be helping someone through their own journey of rediscovery so that they didn't sit in darkness like I had done. To feel someone's energy change and blossom purely by showing them positive representation was deeply gratifying. One woman said to me, 'I now see my stretch marks as my roots that have grown into a tree of life' – something that I will never forget.

I wish I could have told myself that it's normal to get stretch marks and it doesn't only happen when you put on weight, but also when you lose it. Men also get them and some pretty fit men, too. Have you seen those hench men at the gym pulling weights? Have you seen the stretch marks on their arms and legs where their bodies have built muscle? Their stretch marks don't seem to appear to be so unattractive, but on myself as a woman I felt like I was faulty.

Are there products advertised for men to help fade stretch marks, or are they only advertised to pregnant women? I remember feeling pretty embarrassed buying pregnancy stretch-mark cream in the pharmacy when in fact I was just curvy and not, in fact, with child.

My clothes were my shield

Noticing my stretch marks definitely had a big knock-on effect on my confidence. There they were, every time I caught a glimpse of my stomach, reminding me of how I was different to everyone else (or that's how it seemed to me back then). Marked out, literally.

Most of my friends at that time were a lot smaller than me. I was the only one with stretch marks and I hid them very well. I would wear 1950s' petticoats, printed tees, studded leather jackets and have my hair in a beehive, looking like I had walked straight from the set of the John Waters film, *Cry Baby*. If you haven't seen it, it's like the punk version of *Grease* with a young Johnny Depp as the lead and Iggy Pop as his uncle.

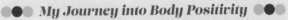

I have to admit I was still using clothing as an armour, like I did growing up in my hometown, but now I felt I had more to hide.

My confidence changed as the layers began to peel off once I was living in London properly as a young adult. The city was diverse, it was full of culture and at last I could say goodbye to the small hometown mentality that was holding me back. There were people here in London who looked like me; they were also finding their own identity and I didn't have to prove my worth to them. I found a group of badass plus-size humans who made me feel like I wasn't an outsider. We supported each other, we hyped each other up and we partied together like there was no tomorrow.

My self-love really grew when I was catapulted into the plus-size modelling scene in 2011 with no clue as to why I was there. I definitely did not predict how it would turn into a multi-billion-pound industry just a few years later.

> **'It was the pressure from society, the pressure to be smaller than I actually was.'**

You know what is so funny? I'm going to tell you a story here about how I started as a plus-size model and what mistakes I made, purely because I was embarrassed about my size and confused as to how I had managed to get myself in front of the camera in the first place.

I lied on my first-ever modelling job because I was ashamed about my size and I didn't understand why I was in this position, shooting with such a prestigious photographer. It's actually quite sad looking back on it now. To be honest, it wasn't really my own thoughts that made me create those lies; it was the pressure from society, the pressure to be smaller than I actually was. Because I knew that was deemed by many to be more desirable.

Beginning my journey

I'll start from the beginning.

My name is Felicity Hayward: I have no middle name as apparently there are already enough syllables in my name. I'm from a small English market town called Bury St Edmunds in Suffolk.

Believe it or not, I'm not naturally blonde and I started dyeing my hair at home (very badly) when I was 14. Around the same time I cut my hair into a mullet as I wanted to look like Rod Stewart; although I loved old-school Hollywood glamour, my style icon always has been, and always will be, Rod.

I moved to London when I was 17 and, at 18, I started studying photography at university. I've always been interested in documenting moments; my grandad Geoff was never without a camera when I was younger and saw himself as a bit of a professional, playing with exposures and different film techniques, so I guess that's where my love for the arts came from.

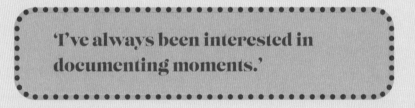

'I've always been interested in documenting moments.'

I enjoyed my time at university, but didn't find my course or the people on it very inspiring. I got a part-time job at a factory processing textile waste (you know, the contents of those recycling bins you might see around your area where you dump

your unwanted wardrobe). The job was to sort the items and source vintage clothing that could be rescued and resold. This led to me running a vintage store in Brick Lane, East London.

There was a moment at that factory that changed my whole view on photography. When we were working on the factory belt, the machinery would offload the huge recycling tanks and we would rummage through pieces, picking out the good items based on their material and labels. Often, though, people would throw their waste into these bins, too. It was pretty disgusting at times and I don't even want to mention half the things we would see, but if there was ever any paper or plastic coming through it would be thrown into the bins underneath. One

morning this battered burgundy photo album came along the belt and inside was just one photo, a sepia 1940s' postcard of the most beautiful woman. I was in awe of her. My mind began to fill with stories about who this person was, the life she had led and why this photo had been dumped in the rubbish.

I then began my journey of collecting old imagery that had been thrown out or lost, and I created my own version of the lost family album and incorporated this into my university work. I fell back in love with photography again, but this time I decided to stop taking new images. After all, why take any more photographs when there are so many beautiful pieces of history that already exist and should be restored?

> 'Old photos held a particular resonance for my family.'

Old photos held a particular resonance for my family. My auntie Maxine had passed away when she was three years old and the loss had devastated my grandparents. She was their first-born and all their photographs of her had been kept locked in the attic for decades. Even my mum hadn't seen them. I didn't want the time for us to see these images as a family to be when some people were no longer with us, so during my degree I made it my mission to create a safe environment that would allow my nan to see the importance of family history. It was a piece of immersive art, if you like. For our second-year university show I didn't opt for a prints-on-the-wall style exhibition. Instead I had a model dressed in 1940s' attire, in a

'A photo is essentially a poem in an image.'

space decorated just as I imagined my nan's living room was when she was growing up, full of vintage trinkets, post-war homeware and an old record player playing Frank Sinatra songs. The model was wearing a dress made from fabric printed with the sepia image of the beautiful woman I found in the factory, and she was hanging up old family images on the wall.

My mother and auntie brought my nan to the exhibition. She sat there in the interactive space, looking at all these lost images from family albums from all over the world and without any of us asking she said, 'I understand. I'm ready. I'll get the photos down from the attic.' This was a really beautiful moment for our family and one we will cherish forever. We got the stories direct from our grandparents; a few weeks later the albums were in their living room, we were all sitting cross-legged on the floor and our grandad instantly turned into the showman he once was (he was a commentator for motorbike racing in the 1950s) and began cranking the lever on the old slide projector, explaining every image to us all in great theatrical detail. It was truly amazing.

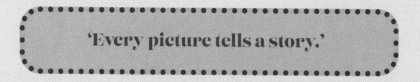

'Every picture tells a story.'

The reason I am telling you all this is because these events really made me dig deeper into my understanding of why we take photographs and document memories and how important these images are. In a time before everything was digital, photographic prints were the only real physical objects we could keep to cherish and use to look back on times that brought us joy. They had a real presence and power. In the words of Rod Stewart (I knew I would get to mention him in the book more than once) – taken from one of my favourite songs that my dad and I would sing to each other (counting the 23 times Rod uses the phrase) – 'Every Picture Tells A Story'.

That is nothing but the truth. Photography is a form of storytelling; a photo is essentially a poem in an image. I wanted my university work to keep pushing this narrative and idea. Little did I know that my future would still involve the camera so many years down the line, but instead of being behind the lens creating a story, I would be in front of it explaining my own journey. At first this was not done so much with words, but simply the size of my body itself would do all the talking. I now know this is a powerful way to get a message across.

I came out of university with a first-class honours degree in photography, but I wasn't sure where my career was going. I was still working at the factory sourcing vintage clothing, as well as working at a pub some evenings and running disco events once a month, just doing whatever I could to afford to live in London.

I then decided I wanted to teach. I felt my degree had such a beautiful narrative to it and this was something I could go back into. I applied to 30 schools in East London and only two got back to me. I started doing work experience in Bow, at a primary school for boys who required special accommodation outside the mainstream. I can still say to this day that it was one of my favourite and most rewarding jobs. I would do 8am to 3pm at the school, then 4pm to midnight as a barmaid so I could pay my rent. Eventually I was offered a teaching assistant role, which led to a full-time teaching scholarship.

A night that changed everything

It was one Saturday night in 2011 when I was down the pub that changed everything. I was dancing in head-to-toe sequins to a Diana Ross record and was approached to do a shoot posing as the late, great Anna Nicole Smith.

The shoot was for a magazine called *Ponystep* and the photographer was Miles Aldridge. I knew his work, it was legendary (he has shot Jarvis Cocker, Joan Collins and David Lynch, to name a few) but if I'm completely honest with you I just thought, well, my nan would think this is quite fancy and I can't wait to see her face when I'm in a fashion magazine shooting with the big dogs.

I wondered how on earth I had got myself in this position. Pot luck presumably: the right place, the right time. But it must be a gimmick, a one-off, surely?

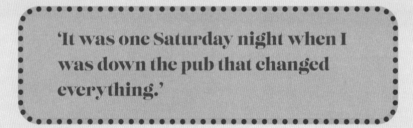

'It was one Saturday night when I was down the pub that changed everything.'

Little did I know that a decade later this would be my full-time job and I would have to leave the teaching role. Not long after the Miles Aldridge shoot, my second life-changing moment occurred. I was still working at a bar in the evenings to get by and this night I was in charge of the speed-dating event upstairs. You weren't allowed your phone behind the bar, a rule that I always ignored. So when I got an email from a modelling agency, I managed to read it sneakily between pulling pints.

It was sent by someone called Siobhan Donaghy, and she was asking me if I already had representation. As if! She then went on to ask me if I wanted to come in and meet the head of their brand-new Curve division, because she thought I might be a perfect fit for their plans.

When I googled her name, it turned out Siobhan was one of the original Sugababes, now working at a model agency on the side. The whole thing seemed very surreal and I honestly believed I was being pranked. This couldn't be real, surely?

I knew I had been shot by Miles Aldridge, but that was a one-off; it was because I was a curvy blonde and the story was about Anna Nicole Smith who I kind of looked like. That was my 15 minutes of fame and nothing more was going to come of it, right? I was confused.

If you don't see representation for yourself in an industry to which you feel constant pressure to conform, why would you even register it as a possibility?

But it was really happening. In November 2011, I was signed as one of the first plus-size models of my age in the UK and that's how it all began. I genuinely didn't think it would go very far so I kept my teaching role at the school in order to have a stable income for my rent.

My fellow teachers and I would do lots of extra-curricular activities for the children at the school. Most of the pupils were from low-income housing and never got the chance to do things outside of their homes, so we would take them to art clubs and football matches on the weekends and we also took them camping in Epping Forest.

I remember one day while I was camping with the school, I got a call from my then agent saying I had been put on option for *Playboy*. I honestly didn't know what to do. This could have been a huge opportunity for me as a model. It would have made my name: I don't think they had used a plus-size non-celebrity model back then. But it would also mean I would have to quit my job.

'I ended up turning down *Playboy*.'

I ended up turning down *Playboy* as it was being photographed by a certain well-known male photographer of the time and I didn't have a good feeling about him. I was later proved right, when he became the subject of a police investigation for several sexual assault offences. A reminder to always listen to your intuition.

No looking back

I loved my job teaching; it was so rewarding. I was looking after children with autism and I was training to become a special educational needs (SEN) teacher, but castings and options kept creeping in and I took the decision to finally leave the profession, not knowing if I could ever come back to it. Not only was it stressful juggling the two careers, but it wasn't fair on the autistic children who I was looking after. They needed a stable teacher more than ever, someone who wasn't having to run off to castings and jobs at the drop of a hat. Routine was such a big part of that role and I was beginning to mess up their schedule with my modelling commitments.

It was a really tough decision, but an obvious one at the same time. I left the school, walking away from a full teaching scholarship. My parents thought I was stupid, but there was something deep within me that felt like this could really become the beginning of a whole new unknown chapter.

I think people forget that back in 2011 plus-size didn't really exist on the UK high street. There were hardly any commercial brands using plus-size models, so the majority of my work was editorial. To explain a little more:

Commercial: This is modelling to endorse brands or companies, for example high-street clothing companies, beauty brands or food and drink products. This is where the money is in modelling, but in 2011 these jobs were few and far between for curvy women.

Editorial: This is when you pose for fashion, press or music publications, such as *Cosmo*, *Glamour*, *i-D* magazine or *Vogue*. There is little to no money in modelling for these publications. It is seen as press for you, so you are lucky to be featured. I was working a lot in editorial at the time, but I still felt like I was the token curvy girl. Plus I was always being asked to be photographed nude: quite frankly we plus-size models were hard to style because there were still not many fashion options for us in those days.

So here's me, with my chubby belly, thick thighs and wobbly bum looking for work, wanting to be part of the industry, but essentially only working on the editorial side with a sad-looking bank balance.

> **'I had this fire in my belly that I wanted to make a difference within the fashion industry.'**

Prime example: in 2012, London hosted the Olympics. I lived in East London. My landlord decided to kick me and my flatmates out so he could rent out our house for more money during that time. My best friend and I found a new place, above a pub in Stepney Green just around the corner from our old flat, but the only thing is, we were broke. We couldn't afford a removal van so we 'borrowed' a shopping trolley from our local supermarket and moved our belongings to our new spot.

I'd quit my teaching role – my only stable income – and I was struggling financially. I had this fire in my belly that I wanted to make a difference within the fashion industry. I knew it wasn't going to happen overnight, but it was a fight I was prepared to risk my previous career for. I knew I would be the token 'plus girl', the one that would often have to wear very little to make a statement for certain brands or publications, but I wanted to see how far the gimmick would go. Would people eventually start to get bored of this agenda or would pioneers like me lead the industry into a new world where curvier models became a normality?

Only time would tell. But for now, there I was, dragging my belongings round the streets of East London. In all fairness, I must have looked like a walking car boot sale – the trolley was piled high with my record player, a mannequin head and a bunch of sequin jackets. I was literally still in the middle of the move when I got an alert on my phone from Twitter. The tweet was brief and to the point: 'i-D Showbiz Issue, Cover Star @ felicityhayward'.

Excuse me!? There I was pushing a shopping trolley with my best mate to our new flat, broke as hell, but now I was the cover star of *i-D* magazine! I remember bursting into tears of happiness and confusion. I had done a shoot for them a few weeks back with no mention of me being on the cover, so it was a total surprise. This was the moment when my confidence really started to grow.

My friends went crazy for the magazine and it blew up online. Girls that looked like me didn't get put on these platforms and in these spaces. My body positivity was born from the love of the friends and family around me and the support from strangers online; that's when I knew I was going to do my absolute best to try to get our big old booties in the same space as our smaller counterparts. It was about time.

Although it was scary to leave my teaching role to pursue fashion, the ethos of teaching would still be in my soul and would carry on with me. So, in 2015, I set up my own body positive movement, 'Self-Love Brings Beauty'.

The main reason as to why I set this up was because of the frustration I felt after one of my biggest interviews. I had just become one of the faces of MAC Cosmetics. I was very lucky because Miles Aldridge was extremely loyal to me at the start of my career; he booked me as a model three times in my first year, something for which, as a plus-size woman, I will always be very grateful.

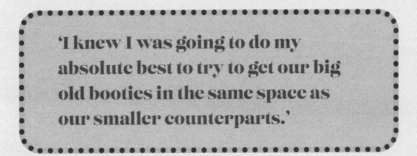

'I knew I was going to do my absolute best to try to get our big old booties in the same space as our smaller counterparts.'

The first booking was, of course, my very first modelling job posing for a story about Anna Nicole Smith, the second was in an East London boozer, posing as a pub landlady serving pints to Cara Delevingne (the irony was that at the time I was genuinely still working this job on the side to pay my rent!) and the third was the MAC Cosmetics campaign.

I remember being on set for the cosmetics shoot. Val Garland was doing the make-up and I let her bleach my eyebrows. I later told her to not re-dye them as I was going out clubbing with the American trans icon Amanda Lepore that evening and I felt colouring them in with pink eye shadow was going to be a fab look for an evening of disco dancing. It was all happening so fast. The images came out and I was being interviewed and all I wanted to do was tell my story and celebrate the fact that curve models were finally being used in beauty campaigns, but all the journalist wanted to ask was, 'So how often do you go to the gym? What is your diet like? Do you calorie count?'

Are these the type of questions you ask someone who has just fronted a celebratory campaign for diversity? Or are they being asked because, quite frankly, the journalist can't fathom why someone like me has been given this opportunity and isn't bothering to hide their disbelief? To be honest, I was still learning myself, but I knew that those questions wouldn't have been asked of someone who was of a standard model size. I felt

'I want the self-love to trickle down.'

like I was being low-key trolled, when really it was the journalist's own insecurities that were being pushed onto me.

This happened a lot in interviews and it made me wonder: if these people had self-love within themselves, if they understood that everyone is beautiful in their own right, maybe they could understand that self-love brings beauty?

And that was it, my little lightbulb moment.

If I could create a space, a hashtag, a movement that could make a difference even to one person's life, then this idea would have been successful. I wanted the self-love to trickle down to the uneducated people pushing their insecurities on me in interviews so it didn't happen to others.

I wanted to create a safe space where everyone felt appreciated, loved and accepted, much like the gang of friends I created when I was exploring London.

I guess the anxiety of leaving my teaching role in the school had kind of come full circle here. I may have not been teaching children, but I was trying to educate others about appreciating each other's differences and celebrating our quirks. It felt natural and rewarding.

I essentially became the role model that my younger self needed and created a space with Self-Love Brings Beauty that made sure others weren't left behind. It was teaching, but on a much larger scale than what I was doing in the classroom.

The whole journey has been a rollercoaster and even just writing about it now I'm getting emotional. Throwing myself in at the deep end into the fashion industry where initially plus-size modelling didn't even exist in the UK was a whirlwind of emotion in itself.

But the reason I'm telling you all of this is because as mentioned earlier, I wasn't always confident. I used to listen to what society told me about conventional beauty. I was embarrassed about my stretch marks and my weight gain because I didn't look like the women in magazines, on the television or in the movies. But ten years later I can honestly say I am so incredibly proud to be one of the first of my age who did finally get onto the cover of those magazines, fronted those beauty campaigns and made way for many more generations of beautiful, non-conforming models to show what representation should really look like.

Achieving genuine body positivity takes time. When I started out, I was ashamed of my measurements, ashamed I didn't fit into most high-street clothing, and, if I was lucky enough to find something, I was always a different size each time and that itself played with my emotions. As I mentioned earlier, I even lied to the stylist of the first shoot I ever did with Miles Aldridge. I gave her smaller measurements than I actually was, as I wanted to appear cooler/more desirable/more fashionable or whatever else was running through my head at that time.

> **'Achieving genuine body positivity takes time.'**

Obviously, I arrived on set and those garments didn't fit and I was even more embarrassed than if I had just given my correct measurements to begin with. I look back on that now and can't believe how backwards that was. If I hadn't been ashamed that I was curvier then I could have had the most incredible custom-sized piece going, but I lied and missed the opportunity. What was I thinking? Did I think I was going to miraculously fit into those clothes when I arrived on set?

You also have to remember that I hadn't seen any plus-size models of my age in the UK at that time. There was Sophie Dahl who was a UK size 12/14 (US size 8/10) at a push and of course she was a celebrity so it didn't really feel like she was relatable to me at the time.

But it all ended well: I did the shoot with Miles, the images were incredible and it was only two weeks after they had been released that I was signed to my agent. Thing were starting to take off.

Fighting for acceptance

I'm not going to say it was always easy from then on. I felt like a gimmick for a long time. I would turn up to castings and 99 per cent of the time I would be the only curve model there. I can safely say the smaller-size models rarely made me feel comfortable sitting in those dull rooms waiting to see the casting director.

> **'I knew that the only reason I got asked if I was the cleaner or in production was because of my size.'**

Back then I despised it, but looking back now I understand most of those girls would have been going through their own insecurities, their own body images issues. Society had forced them to believe that only one type of body was the right type – tall and slender – so why was *I* in the room?

At the end of the day, we are all fighting the same cause, all wanting to be treated equal in society, in fashion and in the media. But back then, only one real beauty type was seen.

It wasn't just castings either. I remember times when I've been on set on a job when a similar situation has occurred.

When you are a model, you usually have to turn up to set make-up free with nude nails and comfy clothes that don't leave any marks on your skin, such as jeans or socks. So most of the time you are turning up completely bare-faced and in your loose pyjamas.

There has been more than one occasion I've turned up to set and been asked by someone in the production crew to take out the bins, or asked by the hair and make-up team to go get them a coffee.

Although I can look back on this now and laugh, I was coming to the set as an established model and I knew that the only reason I got asked if I was the cleaner or in production was because of my size. The thinking went: surely a plus-size woman wouldn't be coming into hair and make-up as a model, so she must be part of the crew? Sorry, babes, I'm actually fronting the campaign.

What is wild is that this same energy for not accepting bigger women in fashion has kind of gone full circle. Body positivity is at the forefront of change and we are now being praised on set for our size. But the change isn't always what it's made out to be; a lot of the time the body positivity is a façade and we only see it because it's now on trend. In the next chapter we'll dig deeper into this ...

Body Image and Toxic Influence

Let's start with a little questionnaire:

1. On a scale of 1 to 10, with 1 being the most negative and 10 being the most positive, how do you feel about your body?
2. Do you think your number would be different if social media didn't exist?
3. What is your favourite part of your body and why?
4. What is your least favourite part of your body and why?
5. Did you choose the answer to number 4 because you are comparing yourself to other people on/offline?
6. How beautiful do you think your best friend is, on a scale of 1 to 10?
7. What are their best attributes?
8. Would you say the same about yourself?

Even as I'm writing this and I'm imagining you reading this book and processing these answers in your head, I have a feeling that the majority of you will say fewer positive things about yourself than you would about your best friend. When we think of others we think about their whole persona – their aura, their laugh, their kindness and their strength, as well as their appearance – but when we think of ourselves, why are we always so quick to dismiss the good things about our bodies? Why are we always so fixated on the 'negatives'?

Let's get into the root cause here; let's look into the impact that societal pressures play on our perceptions of our bodies and let's dig deep into why we don't speak as kindly to ourselves as we do to our loved ones. But let's start by looking at the body positivity movement and how it came about.

The origins of the body positivity movement

The term 'body positivity' has only become popularized in the last decade with the rise of social media, but the movement actually began in 1969 after a New York engineer called Bill Fabrey saw his wife get mistreated because of her size. Fabrey created the NAAFA (The National Association to Advance Fat Acceptance) at around the same time as a group of feminists in California created the Fat Underground movement, releasing their very own *Fat Liberation Manifesto* in 1973 that demanded equal rights for fat people in all areas of life. Nothing much came of this for 20 years, then later on, in 1996, an organization called The Body Positive was founded by Elizabeth

> 'Black women have had a particular challenge in the way their bodies are viewed and represented.'

Scott and Connie Sobczak, which aims to support those seeking freedom for people perpetually struggling with their bodies and is still going strong today. Slowly, the idea of body positivity started to take root.

Black women, of course, have had a particular challenge in the way their bodies are viewed and represented, and they often get written out of the history of the body positive narrative. Yet Black women have always played an important role in standing up for marginalized bodies and those often ignored by mainstream beauty standards. The predominantly white body positive movement for years perpetuated the myth that the Black community was more accepting of plus-size people, and could therefore be excluded from this kind of activism. According to *Zenerations*,[1] Margaret K. Bass was one of the first women of colour to draw attention to this double standard with her essay 'On Being a Fat Black Girl in a Fat-Hating Culture', first published in 2000, in which she wrote about her experiences growing up in the segregated South during the 1950s and 1960s and the discrimination and self-loathing she endured. She paved the way for other women of colour to reclaim their bodies and learn to love themselves.

Nowadays, happily, things are starting to change, and body positivity influencers of all races and colours are becoming more prominent. Today, racial inclusiveness is an essential part of the movement. There are also big improvements in terms of creating a welcoming environment for people of the LGBTQ+ community, emphasizing the fact that body positivity should be a space for all – although of course there is always more work to be done until there is full representation and inclusivity for everyone.

> 'Body positivity should be a space for all.'

1 'The Black History of the Body Positive Movement', Briana Dominici, www.zenerations.org

What is body positivity and how can we learn to love ourselves unapologetically?

To me, body positivity is finding a balance between your positive and negative thoughts.

It's about finding a middle ground between what we have been told to believe, according to the industry standard of beauty, and believing your own hype. It's about finding a calmness in your mind, body and soul. It's about learning to love yourself for exactly who you are right now and who you will continue to grow to be. No matter if that growth includes changes that society deem to be negative, such as changes in skin texture, hair loss, weight fluctuations or marks on your skin. It's finding the acceptance that change is okay and completely normal.

> **'Change is okay and completely normal.'**

It's also about understanding that this feeling of inner peace isn't something that just magically appears and stays with you all the time. We all have bad days. Even as I'm writing this today I am in such a grumpy mood; I haven't got dressed, my hair is tied up in a giant scrunchie and I'm eating a half-empty pot of hummus with a spoon, followed by a blackcurrant ice lolly chaser. I'm so far behind on work deadlines and I've just

SELF LOVE

realized I'm only wearing one sock. It's 3.49pm and, quite frankly, I'm not feeling myself. It could be to do with the weather, the moon, my hormones or simply the fact we don't have to be happy with ourselves every day. Sometimes you feel a thousand dollars and look like a snack in your new fancy sequin outfit and other times you have one sock on and you are now eating all the leftovers available in the fridge. Life is about balance.

Body positivity is a journey with many pit stops on the way and I hope you see this book like a lunch date at an old-school roadside diner, with every chapter a new dish that leaves you feeling full and nourished, but with room to take a slice of apple pie home with you after each sitting.

Insecurity starts young

Body image issues often seem to start young, even when we don't realize they're being played out as part of our narrative. Girls, in particular, are expected to look and behave a certain way from a very young age, and sometimes even well-meaning family members can say things that make kids internalize negative feelings about their bodies without them even realizing it's happening. Think about the so-called 'harmless' comments that are often overheard from parents or guardians, older siblings or teachers and absorbed by the children around them. Think of how many people talk about drinking 'fat Coke', consuming 'naughty food' or having a 'cheat day'. Or how often we are negative about our body shapes, say we can only wear items of clothing that we deem to be flattering, or compare

> **'Isn't it obvious that children can absorb negativity coming from us when we speak about our bodies with disregard?'**

ourselves to others. You know when you meet a person for the first time you can sometimes tell instantly that their energy is off; you can literally feel that they are unhappy about themselves? Isn't it obvious that children can absorb the same negativity coming from us when we speak about our bodies with a similar disregard? How could this internalized negativity not slowly become part of their worldview and go on to influence what they believe to be normal?

In 2016, a study by the Professional Association for Childcare and Early Years found out that nearly one-quarter of childcare workers saw body image issues in children between the ages of three and five years old. Yes, you heard that right, even before they have properly started school, there are children already internalizing negative feelings about their bodies, when quite frankly they should be completely carefree at that age. The age when anxiety is starting to disturb children's minds is getting lower every year. How upsetting is that?

> **'It's no wonder that so many children struggle with self-esteem.'**

These children grow up to be teenagers and then social media gets added to the mix. These kids will already have internalized all the negative wording around body image they have heard from family members and their peers at school, and unconsciously noted the lack of any real diversity in television shows, adverts and magazines ... and now they have an online platform where all of the above is magnified and accessible to them on a much larger scale! It's no wonder that so many children struggle with self-esteem and self-image.

It doesn't help that social media platforms are overwhelmed by advertisements and promotions. It doesn't help that it's a known fact that our smartphones can track what we have been searching online or talking about. You know when you mention you are looking for a 1970s' shag rug or have googled how to get candle wax out of your favourite sweater and suddenly there are swipe-up links with the items needed to buy or fix those very things? Well, imagine you are a teen and constantly hearing about diet culture from your elders; you've looked online at what they were talking about and suddenly you have fat-burning gummies in the shape of a cute bunny being offered on your feed. The power of words is dangerous and it's so important to make sure we aren't feeding the minds of our younger generation with the things we have had to unlearn as adults and quite frankly are still trying to navigate ourselves.

Facing up to the mean girls

I wasn't the popular girl in school. I was the little grunge kid with weird clothes; the one who got picked last in sports class and the one who didn't get a prom date.

I'll tell you this for free: school or high school is almost always an inverse mirror to real life – so often the shiniest, the most manipulative or the most forceful characters crown themselves the royalty of the scene. But then adult life happens and with it comes the realization that what you really need is grit and character to make a success of yourself in the real world.

> **'What you really need is grit and character to make a success of yourself in the real world.'**

There was a moment for me when I finally understood this. I was back home at Christmas; I had just finished working on my first-ever big commercial job with a high-street retailer and they had recently opened a store in my hometown. I was excited because it was somewhere my nan could go easily and I was so happy she could see that all my hard work had reached as far as Suffolk. The funny thing is, I was fronting this big campaign and there were posters of my image up in all the stores, but I hadn't been paid for it yet. Sometimes these big jobs can take up to 90 days to pay and that is the industry standard, unfortunately. So there I was, back home on a festive night out and one of the popular girls from my school approached me at the bar.

'Oh my goodness, it's SO nice to see you,' she said. (Let's just say this girl wasn't nice to me in school and had never spoken to me like this before.) 'Me and my friends have seen you in the store and we would love to know more!'

At this point I asked the barmaid what Champagne they had.

'Bollinger is the only one we have left,' she replied.

'That will do,' I said, knowing full well I didn't have much in my bank account, but I was trying to make a point here. I entered my PIN number and by some luck of the gods it went through. The girl and her friends all came over, excited that I had bought them a bottle for us to share to celebrate the fact that I, the chubby weirdo from school, was the face of the shop they all frequented.

'How many glasses?' asked the barmaid.

'Oh, this straw will do,' I replied.

And with that I grabbed the bottle, wished the girls Merry Christmas and walked off with adrenaline coursing through me, channelling the energy of all the kids at school who had ever felt the negativity of this group of girls' presence.

'As women
we really
should be
lifting each
other up.'

Although getting one over on these girls certainly felt like a long-awaited personal triumph, given how mean they were to me when I was younger, I'm aware things are never black and white. The reality is, those girls were probably as unhappy as me when we were at school. Everyone has insecurities, even those who won the body trend lottery back then. And if we're honest, I now make a career from my curves, so maybe the tides have turned!

> **'How amazing it would be if, as women, we could just ally together no matter our differences.'**

That said, sometimes you have to ask yourself who is really to blame for these body image pressures. It's often other girls who make us feel bad about ourselves, whether at school or on social media. As women we really should be lifting each other up. It's quite sad when you have experienced these things and you look back, as it feels like these women were simply deflecting their own insecurities and acting out their own pressure to fit into the cookie-cutter beauty ideal of the time. How amazing it would be if, as women, we could just ally together no matter our differences, no matter what society is telling us about what we should look like, and stick a big middle finger up to whoever is trying to control our beauty ideals! It's only by sticking together that we will break this negative cycle of comparison and force a change of attitude in wider society as a whole.

Although it did feel like some sort of victory by sipping that Champagne through one measly little straw in front of my old classmates, the reality is that it could have been a beautiful moment of celebration for the women of my small hometown that one of us had left for London and hit a little milestone. We could have chatted about their families, the small local businesses they set up; we could have talked about how we could help each other grow; we could have arranged a hangover brunch date or simply sipped and clinked our Champagne glasses together and enjoyed some nostalgic memories from our time at school. And all this didn't happen because one of us had a different measurement around their waist and wasn't accepted by the so-called cool kids at the time.

If only we knew as teens about all the pressures we would have as women in terms of spending our lives conforming to ever-changing body shape trends, maybe we could have rejected it all and enjoyed ourselves a little more freely without any inhibitions or judgements.

A short history of body shapes

I grew up in the 1990s. The poster girls for this generation were Britney and Christina. It was the era of spaghetti-strap mini dresses, metallic eyeshadow, pedal pushers, platform shoes and butterfly clips, all modelled on very small slender frames. That was the look that the majority were aspiring to and the girls above fitted into this body trend aesthetic.

I say a trend because unfortunately it was just that. I would like to show you the timeline of how the desired body shape has changed, and this has only been in the last 100 years – we would need to have a whole new book if you wanted to delve further back in history.

1900s

The Victorians were notorious for their bizarre beauty ideals – the fashionable aesthetic of the time was modelled on the look of those afflicted by tuberculosis, or consumption as it was known then. When you think of a typical Victorian heroine in a Dickens novel you think of a beautiful woman with pale skin, dilated eyes, rosy cheeks and crimson lips – and a fragile, delicate figure with a 16-inch waist, of course. Victorian women would achieve the pale, sickly look by swallowing ammonia or bathing in arsenic – even though they knew these substances were poisonous – and the tiny waist would be accomplished by squeezing themselves into dangerously tight corsets. No wonder Victorian women were always fainting and had to be revived with smelling salts.

An even more horrific genuine Victorian 'solution' for achieving a fashionably tiny waist was the tapeworm diet.

At heart, it was very simple: the woman would ingest pills that contained tapeworm eggs, then when the eggs hatched inside of them, the parasites would grow and absorb all of the host's nutrients. The rumoured benefit was that you would continue losing weight however much you ate.

Of course, it was risky in many ways. Not only can tapeworms grow up to 9m (30ft) in length, but they can also cause many illnesses including headaches, eye problems, meningitis, epilepsy and dementia. But beauty is pain, right? We must all make sacrifices to look our best – even inviting huge worms to grow inside us?!

No words, honestly.

1920s

Enter the era of the Great Gatsby and the Flapper Girl. Now the desired frame is a very slender, elongated physique, elegantly bedecked in strings of pearls, lace and fringing.

To help its customers achieve this whippet-framed aesthetic, a well-known cigarette brand promoted a cigarette-only diet to shed the unwanted pounds. The nicotine in cigarettes is, after all, an effective appetite suppressant.

The scary thing is that back in those days, even the *doctors* were pushing the same narrative. Believe it or not, they were actually prescribing cigarettes to patients wanting to lose weight. No matter that even if you did decrease your weight, in later decades it would be discovered that you'd be dramatically *increasing* your risk of lung cancer.

1950s

In comes the old-school Hollywood glam. Marilyn Monroe has become Hollywood's biggest sex symbol and all the attention is

1920s

1950s

1990s

2020s

on her hourglass figure. Pointed and padded triangular bralettes, cinched-in waists and curvaceous clothes are all the rage.

This leads to some new targeted diet ads, but this time for supplements that helped you *gain* weight to be deemed more attractive, with many advertisements showcasing skinnier frames as being undesirable. It has gone full circle now.

1960s

The swinging sixties arrived alongside the model Twiggy with her lean figure, androgynous appearance, colourful psychedelic prints, thick mascara and platform shoes. Long legs, flat chests and a youthful, teenage physique epitomized the fashionable new look. We had gone from the weight-gain pills of the fifties back to pushing a very petite frame once again. I can only imagine the pressures that women must have felt in this decade – going from the curvaceous, hour-glass silhouette of the fifties to the long and lean look of the sixties in just ten years.

1970s

'We've Only Just Begun' by the Carpenters was in the top of the charts at the start of the decade, but sadly the singing duo's journey had a very tragic ending.

Brother and sister Richard and Karen Carpenter were enormously successful in the 1970s but unfortunately it wasn't just their music that gained them headlines. Thin was definitely in at the time, and extreme diets were everywhere. Perhaps the most dangerous was the 'Last Chance Diet' created by Dr Robert Linn in 1976. Dr Linn's bestselling book recommended a liquid diet of only 400 calories a day, to be consumed via a protein drink called Prolinn, which was manufactured from a mixture of various slaughterhouse by-products like hides, bones and hooves. It has been said that up to 60 people died from malnutrition while following this diet.

Like a lot of women in the seventies, Karen Carpenter struggled with body image issues and hired a personal trainer to help her shape up. She was then put onto a carbohydrate-based diet, which naturally caused her to bulk up. She fired her trainer and began to take her own extreme measures to combat the weight gain. She started using laxatives, taking 80 to 90 tablets a night alongside unprescribed thyroid medication to speed up her metabolism.

Unsurprisingly, she was soon diagnosed with anorexia and her condition became well known after public appearances showed her looking gaunt. This was the first real time there had been any media coverage of an eating disorder. Up to this point the only thing women would see in the press were the toxic weight-loss advertisements; now Karen's condition revealed the darker side to what they promoted.

Tragically, anorexia took Karen's life in 1983. She was 32.

1980s

In this decade we have the rise of the supermodel, with Naomi Campbell and Cindy Crawford fronting the fashion industry with their slender, tall and strong figures.

Jane Fonda's aerobic workouts were wildly successful, and women internalized her 'no pain, no gain' mantra. Was it a coincidence that jaw wiring became a procedure for weight loss around the same time? Orthodontic brackets were fixed onto the teeth and wired together so you couldn't eat solid food, only liquids. Some people were known to have this device in their mouths for around nine months. This awful method has, to my horror, suddenly popped up again in a different form in 2021.

1990s

At the dawn of the 1990s, there is a new supermodel in town: the tiny, teenage Kate Moss, who was being regularly called 'the waif' in the press. 'Waif' of course means a young person who is thin and looks unhealthy or uncared for. That was what was being celebrated as 'fashionable' at the time.

This is also the era in which the term 'heroin chic' became popularized.

Before I delve into this, just read those two words again.

Heroin: *a highly addictive drug derived from morphine, often used as a narcotic.*

Chic: *elegantly and stylishly fashionable.*

This phrase had been coined to describe a specific popular look, characterized by an extremely skinny body, prominent bone structure, pale skin, dark-ringed eyes and messy, stringy hair. One of the early adopters of this look was the American supermodel Gia Carangi – only in her case the heroin part of the 'heroin chic' beauty ideal was sadly very literal.

Gia tragically died at the age of 26, and although she was seen as the first-ever supermodel, I find it hard to understand how her struggle with a heroin drug addiction was glamorized and made into a trend that even graced the advertisements of some very big global brands in the 90s.

I want to ask you a question here – would there have been a trend for the first-ever plus-size supermodel if she had struggled with an addiction? For example, imagine a curvy model praised for being the first of her size and breaking boundaries. Imagine if she was also an alcoholic. Imagine she drank to excess and had liver failure. Would being an alcoholic become fashionable?

Or would there be a trend for a plus-size supermodel who became addicted to sugar and died of diabetes? Would 'diabetes chic' become the next new trend, with an insulin-inspired capsule collection?

Of course not; that would be ridiculous. If a person is plus-size, it would be seen as promoting obesity and an unhealthy lifestyle.

But heroin – fine. It's fashion; it's rock 'n' roll baby. An addiction that makes you die quicker but makes you thin in the process – well, that's glamorous.

The issue I have here is there are a lot of people whose sole focus is to push blame onto fat bodies and tell us how damaging we are to the planet, yet we allowed trends like heroin chic to become mainstream, which continue to emphasize the idea that thin is beautiful and healthier and fat is ugly and dangerous.

2000s

Into the new millennium and Giselle Bündchen is crowned the most beautiful woman of the world by *Rolling Stone* magazine. The focus of this era is on lean, 'healthy', slim and toned bodies. Victoria's Secret models seem to epitomize the body trend of the era, but it is no surprise that eating disorders such as anorexia and bulimia are at such high levels.

In 2007, an Italian billboard campaign for fashion brand Nolita fronted by French model Isabelle Caro had her posing nude with her exhaustingly small 58lb (26kg) body on show, highlighting her severe anorexia. Devised as an initiative to raise awareness of the eating disorder, the photoshoot was backed by Livia Turco, the Italian Minister for Health, who wanted to promote responsibility in the fashion industry for the women modelling.

The posters were immediately banned as they were distressing for people to view. They were removed after they were posted all around Milan Fashion Week, but the images went viral online. The photo was very hard to process; Caro looked incredibly ill, skeletal and unhappy, but it did make change. Size zero models were banned on the catwalk by some very big French fashion houses such as LVMH.

Sadly, Caro died in 2010 aged 28.

2010s

Well, hello diversity; I'm so glad you finally arrived in the room. America has seen your plus-size models putting in the work over the last few years, even decades, so it's about time we start to shake this place up over in the UK, too, and try to play catch-up with our USA babes. It's time to really make a change now. It's very much needed; have you seen what's been happening in the last few decades? It's been a mess.

Hello New York and hello to Ashley Graham, Marquita Pring, Liris Crosse, Precious Lee, Candice Huffine, and Elly Mayday (now sadly missed). We've been watching.

Hello Australia and hello to you Robyn Lawley, you absolute babe; and hello Celeste Barber, keep being brilliant.

Hello United Kingdom, thanks for offering me a seat at the table. I didn't know we were trying it like this over here. Let's get this plus-size movement fired up. Let's go, Iskra Lawrence; let's go, Philomena Kwao; let's go, Saffi Karina; let's go, Jada Sezer – we've got some catching up to do.

The hourglass curve figure is now extremely popular, the influence of the Kardashians and their toned, somewhat man-made curves is here and the Instagram baddie aesthetic is now on the rise. The door has been opened to us as thicker women, but let's make sure we show our real side too: the blemishes, the stretch marks, the cellulite and the scars. Let's normalize curvy

> **'Let's make sure we show our real side too: the blemishes, the stretch marks, the cellulite and the scars.'**

bodies so that not one body shape is idealized, or else we will just be going around in circles again.

Where are we now?

Okay, you listened ... kind of. Representation of an increasingly diverse range of body types is now becoming a huge part of many advertising campaigns.

I can see the internal work that has been happening behind the scenes as a model. Back in the early 2010s I could count the number of curvy models of my age in the UK on one hand; now we have hundreds of fantastic fuller-figured models and we are also seeing a rise in the male plus-size industry. Rather than being a small and yet often disregarded 'special' section, we now have agencies dedicated solely to plus-size models and the mainstream agencies have extended their boards, too. We can also celebrate the fact that there are more extended size ranges from high-street retailers that are now accessible to us.

All of this change is welcome, of course. But I realize my viewpoint is blurred. I have seen such a growth within my personal career in terms of opportunities that have become available in modelling, but looking at the industry from the viewpoint of the consumers, that shift of normalizing diversity is still taking its sweet time. I may be thinking that this is great,

we have come on leaps and bounds because I am now modelling for a certain brand that didn't stock our sizes before, but that brand might have decided to sell that range only in a tiny back section of their flagship store, with no promotion or celebration. Then they pull that plus-size section from their physical stores on the high street, because – surprise, surprise – it didn't do well because no one knew about it, leading to it being sold solely online. This leaves the curve customer with a less-than-average shopping experience and pushes the narrative again that being larger means you deserve less than others. You can't have things in real life like your smaller counterparts; you have to buy your clothes online while sitting on your sofas at home.

> **'Are we only starting to be catered for now simply because it's become fashionable to be curvier?'**

It's all a little backwards to say the least. I personally believed we were finally getting there with the growth in the plus-size market, but are those changes in the industry due to a genuine understanding of our needs or is it just a cynical attempt to make profit? Are these changes being made grudgingly or are they being celebrated? And are we only starting to be catered for now simply because it's become fashionable to be curvier?

I naïvely like to think that it will now be this way forever. That our time has finally come to be accepted more within the fashion industry. But I can't help but think that a new trend is going to hit us shortly because we are all starting to love ourselves authentically a little bit too much.

Or is the new trend – **toxic positivity** – already here and we don't even realize it's happening?

When body positivity turns toxic

The term 'body positivity' is on the tip of everyone's tongue, finally! It's a good thing, right?

After all, people are presumably only using the term because they genuinely believe that all bodies are good bodies and should be celebrated? No one is lying about what they truly believe about their body to make monetary gain or get thousands of new followers. However could I think such a thing!

All bodies include tall ladies with small bums, short gals with big bellies, curvy babes with little boobies, right? It includes women of colour, yes? Or are we just going to feature solely the current popular white, hourglass-shaped, plus-size body?

Is the new wave of bo-po hashtagging influencers contorting their bodies to create one small belly roll just a veiled attempt to jump onto the body positivity trend – or do they genuinely believe their Instagram captions and tags?

Of course, you can be body positive at any size; it's a mindset after all and is for everyone. But what I struggle to believe is whether the smaller-framed influencers would be forcefully trying to appear larger and promote body positivity if the term didn't currently have 8.5 million hashtag impressions on Instagram.

I'm not saying everyone is chasing the curve community; there are a lot of genuine people out there trying to make positive change. But just keep an eye on the people who evolve with the next trending tag, the ones who have arrived to claim their Girl Scout bo-po badge and will then move on to the next hashtag once it arrives. Was their whole agenda solely to trick you into engaging in their relatable content? Who knows? Only time will tell.

> **'Keep an eye on the people who evolve with the next trending tag.'**

When you look at the timeline of trends and faddy toxic diets, I can literally feel the weight of the pressures we have had to bear to change our bodies to fit into society's expectations. But who is to blame for this? Is it the women themselves – those lucky ones who happened to have the more desirable body shapes at the time?

I think once you look into the deep-rooted reason body image popularity keeps changing, then you are able to really understand what 'beauty' is and who is controlling it.

What is the one thing that has held together all these popular body trends throughout the decades, the one thing that has always benefited? Is it the humans who have constricted themselves, limited their diets, put themselves under the knife and spent their hard-earned money in order to fit in? Or is it the CEOs, the owners and distributors of all the products, diets, beauty treatments, surgery clinics and clothing companies who have been riding off the back of body image trends to make profits from our insecurities? I think it's pretty obvious what the answer is.

I would also like to be clear at this point that I do not have a problem with people changing the way they look and I do not have a problem with people wanting to change themselves via surgery. The problem I have is when it is done under societal pressure and is not done from the heart or a physical need.

Cosmetic surgery is vital both physically and mentally when people are transitioning to becoming their true selves and it is also vital when someone may have been hurt and needs life-saving surgery in order to heal. Or you could be someone like my mum, who, at the age of 50, decided she wanted to be the best version of herself and had a boob job. The difference being, she wasn't going around lying about whether she'd had it done. She literally went from an A cup to a D cup; she was gladly showing off her new assets and she had it done for herself.

The changes here aren't the issue – changing your body isn't an issue – the only problem I have is when I feel pressure has been forced upon people to change and the influence is coming from someone who isn't telling the truth about what they have had done.

> **'Changing your body isn't an issue.'**

Let's talk about toxic influence

The people who are at the forefront of these pressuring decisions around body change are not so much the popular girls in school these days, but the popular girls on the internet.

At least with the kids at school it was very apparent when someone had had a new haircut, new piercing or had started a new fashion trend. You could see it first-hand; it was real life. But with this new social media world we live in, nothing is exactly what it seems.

I feel the so-called body positive movement, which was initially created to celebrate bodies of all types, has now been hijacked by celebrities and influencers and turned into something more commercial.

People are using the term 'body positive' on their posts as an endorsement; they are praising their newfound love for their bodies – but their bodies aren't real and they are telling you they are. These people lie through their bright white veneers, preaching that everything is natural, when the only natural thing about them is their Whole Foods order. They preach self-love after they have changed their whole body – saying that it's genetics, when it's really all aesthetics – which is very dangerous.

And there are some popular influencers surfing the wave of this trend, with the waves splashing straight into their bank accounts. The ones who overnight have suddenly become curvier versions of themselves: their thighs are bigger, their bums are more peachy, their waists are tiny, their facial features have changed and their lips seem to have become bigger – and yet they want you to believe their altered appearance is only down to a fabulous product that they happen to be selling.

You do you, Boo. Change isn't a bad thing, but when you are in a position of influence – and this holds for every influencer that exists on the World Wide Web – remember the power you hold over your followers, especially the younger generation. Remember, when you are in a position of influence, you should reflect on what you promote to the world and the harm you can and will be causing by lying to your audience. Remember that your followers love and believe you, so if you are promoting a product you don't actually use, you have the chance of putting these people in danger – the very people who, let's face it, bankroll your lifestyle.

> **'Remember the power you hold over your followers.'**

I would categorize myself as a model turned social media 'influencer' but I would never actively promote an item that could cause someone harm. I would never lie about having anything done to my body that could cause others to question themselves and their body image. Sadly, though, not everyone online shares my reservations and beliefs.

Want an example? Recently there was an appetite-suppressant lollipop that was promoted by influencers on social media. Yes, that's right: a lollipop that has chemicals in it to stop you feeling hungry. I don't know about you, but as an adult when I am hungry, I often go for something a bit more substantial than a lollipop as they are generally targeted at kids and teenagers. Now, if you were a global entrepreneur with

'When you are in a position of influence, you should reflect on what you promote to the world.'

millions of followers, and if you were also a mother, would you give these products to your children? If, like me, you think the answer is no, do you think it's right to promote it online to younger siblings, friends or family members? Kids who might not have any guidance and truly believe anything that is in pop culture?

The same goes for all the influencers online who promote those diet drinks that apparently give you the appearance of a flat stomach. Many of these drinks are nothing but chemicals and laxatives that are not meant to be used as meal replacements. We've had women using diet pills and diet teas and actually dying from complications due to the damage these products can cause for your body.

A couple of years back we saw an ad from a well-known protein supplement company, promoting their new weight-loss collection with a very Barbie-esque slender model in a bikini with the caption, 'Are you beach body ready?' This not only objectifies women and is socially irresponsible but again pressurizes us into believing you can only wear a bikini if your body looks like that of this model – and if it doesn't, you need to buy their products to lose weight in order for it to do so.

We also have celebrities and influencers who have had extreme surgeries done to their bodies such as Brazilian butt lifts, liposuction and hip fillers in order to become more curvy. Yet they are leading their followers to believe they've changed their shape solely through dieting and extreme exercising.

The issue I have is there are so many young minds looking online who don't realize these people have gone under the knife for this body image fix. They believe the transformation is achieved by personal trainers and countless hours in the gym, private chefs and faddy supplements.

Not everyone can afford this lifestyle, so many people will attempt much more affordable alternatives, including fad diets, which can easily lead to mental health issues such as eating disorders, as well as exposing them to the physical dangers of extreme dieting.

There have also been cases of young girls going to get illegal surgeries carried out by non-professional doctors in motels in the USA and other countries. The girls are having materials such as cement injected into their bodies and are dying of infection. For what – a body trend?

In 2011, a 20-year-old British student travelled from London to Philadelphia to get injections to enlarge her curves. Silicone was injected into her backside and hips and she later died as the silicone moved to her lungs and stopped her heart. The person who performed the procedure with no medical training went on trial for third-degree murder.

> **'Fad diets can easily lead to mental health issues such as eating disorders.'**

Up until May 2021 there was no legal age limit for dermal fillers in the UK. A law has now passed that no under-18s will be able to get Botox or fillers under the new legislation. This is good news, obviously, but what still scares me is that the industry is largely unregulated, meaning anyone can legally provide injectable treatments. So people over the age of 18 can still get these treatments done in the UK by just about anyone, without a need for registration or medical qualifications. Even with all the horror stories we are hearing about, this still hasn't changed.

Over in the USA you have to be over 21 years old to get fillers according to the FDA (Food and Drug Administration). But there are no specific laws in the US that prevent teenagers from getting cosmetic surgery. So any under-18s can go under the knife, according to the ASPS (the American Society of Plastic Surgeons), as long as they have parental consent.

Aside from this, we now seem to be going back in time to the eighties with the jaw-wiring weight-loss technique making a guest appearance once again. The new version of this involves medical professionals putting magnets into women's mouths. The idea is that they fit them to your top and lower teeth so you can only open your jaw 2mm (⅛in). This is to stop you eating any solid food so that you are only able to have a liquid diet until a specific amount of weight has been lost. In the words of the professor who invented this, having your mouth essentially locked shut is 'a non-invasive, reversible, economical and attractive alternative to surgical procedures'.

A literal magnet in your mouth to stop you eating food! We need food to survive, to fuel our bodies, to bring us together and to give us variety and joy in our lives, and we are now having medical professionals tell us that this extreme procedure is an 'attractive' way to lose weight?

I'm not a doctor, but from my experience as a human being, I can safely say I believe that forcing someone to eat only liquids for a number of weeks for a quick weight-loss fix is essentially another version of a fad diet, and you can bet your bottom dollar that it would lead straight back into eating normal solid food after this traumatic experience was over. What if the person needed to be sick? Would they choke to death? What if the person was having a heart attack and needed medical assistance? And how would you even brush your teeth? The whole process sounds both pointless and harmful.

Let me make an alternative suggestion. What if the money used in the research of this absurd procedure had been used to teach children in schools about having a healthy relationship with food and understanding its nutritional value?

Now wouldn't that be a radical idea?

How we are influenced by other people

I'd like to end this chapter by asking you to answer a few questions. Please answer honestly; this is your book and no one is judging.

Please tick the following.

1. Growing up as a child, if you were to see your parent/ guardian with a magnet in their mouth stopping them from eating, do you think this would make you feel guilty about eating solid foods? **Y/N**
2. Do you think this would have an adverse effect on your relationship with food growing up? **Y/N**
3. Do you think you would start to see food as the enemy and not as fuel needed to survive? **Y/N**
4. Would you start viewing your clothing size in a negative way? **Y/N**

5. If you saw this procedure being advertised by a social media influencer or medical professional would you be tempted to try it? **Y/N**

If you have answered yes to any of the above answers, I think we both know there is definitely a problem with the way things are advertised to us.

We have literally been shamed, gaslighted, bullied, humiliated and lied to, not only by the diet industry, but also the online influencers, celebrities and even our medical advisors. People are finally waking up to these obnoxious money-making companies and ideals.

When you look at the timeline of trends and procedures over the last 100 years, you can understand why it's been a turbulent ride for so many people. Now that the phrase 'body positivity' is on everyone's lips, we need to make sure this decade and future decades to come are filled with change, understanding and truth. We need to differentiate between genuine body positivity and toxic influence; and we need to celebrate the former and call out the latter. This is our moment. And you can start by changing the way you think about yourself in relation to others.

> **'Start by changing the way you think about yourself in relation to others.'**

Ditch the Comparison

We've all been there: I wish I had that body, that outfit, that job, that relationship or that holiday. The temptation of comparison is literally in our faces daily, even more so now that social media is one of our main sources of information. Everything and everyone are now accessible, which can be both a good and a bad thing.

> **'Comparison is the highjacker of positive thoughts.'**

Yes, we can now see the representation online that some of us may not have grown up with, but alongside this there is the danger of falling prey to comparison culture, which is when we compare ourselves to other people – whether it's their lifestyle, looks, wealth, health or body shape. Being surrounded by

popular culture, we can't help but absorb what is deemed to be the best way to look and live our lives and it's almost impossible not to wonder how we can achieve this for ourselves.

We are all guilty of feeling like this in some shape or form whether we realize it or not. It's virtually inescapable. We are being pushed by propaganda that is fuelled by the establishments, companies and platforms that use this comparison culture not only to control us, our thoughts and the way we see ourselves, but also, once again, to make money for themselves.

A comparison challenge

Try answering some of these questions to suss out how good you are at resisting comparisons that may negatively affect your mindset:

- Do you feel that your body shape is represented in high-street fashion or when you are shopping online?

- How do you feel when you are shopping for clothes online and the model is a completely different shape and size to you?

- How do you feel when you are shopping with friends and can't find your size in-store?

- How do you view influencers and celebrities who show off their 'perfect' bodies?

Comparison culture damage

I know I personally feel the most body confident in a leopard-print catsuit, platform boots, big gold hoops and a bold lippie these days, but that hasn't always been the case. It was comparison culture that tried to kill my confidence when I was younger. Everywhere I looked – among my friends, in the high-street clothes shops, in the fashion magazines I read – I was made to feel inadequate.

It's strange because, looking back, I was the biggest one in my friendship group, but on a bigger scale (excuse the pun), I was really only the UK average size for a woman – it was just the fact that I was still a teenager that made me stand out. I had constant reminders that I should hide my big bum, cover my hips and wear big, baggy, alternative clothing.

The problem is, the gossip magazines back when I was growing up were depicting bikini-clad female celebrities who had been papped on holiday being shamed as walking heart attacks because they had gone from a UK size 8 (US size 4) to a UK size 14 (US size 10). My mum would get these magazines and because they were around the house I would start to believe that there was something wrong with me if I was the same size or bigger than the women who were featured in these publications.

The small market town I grew up in had limited choices on the high street and was even more restricted by the size ranges they carried when I was a teen. I never experienced that enjoyment of feeling part of a fashion trend or being able to dress the same way as my friends. I had to look in the 'older' department for my clothes or not have the pieces at all.

Saturday mornings were a girls' shopping ritual in my town. I remember one week in particular I had been invited by some of the more popular girls in school to join them. I was so excited. I got dressed super early and walked into town with my CD Walkman listening to Linkin Park's *Hybrid Theory*, ready to meet the girls outside Woolworths. Pedal pushers were in fashion at the time, the mid-calf-length trouser with a tight fit that often came in a range of fun colours. It was a very popular style in the fifties and sixties that had a resurfaced as a fashion in the late nineties. Everyone wanted them and it was no surprise that we made straight for a very popular high-street store to find the latest ones on offer.

> **'I couldn't help but compare myself to others and find myself wanting.'**

The rest of the girls all found a pair in their size, but unfortunately there weren't any in mine. Back then the stores only ever stocked a very small number of the largest size, which I often wouldn't even fit in. Sometimes, if I was lucky and the fabric was stretchy or it was an oversized cut, I would be able to buy something, but nine times out of ten I wasn't.

Everyone got a pair of pedal pushers that day except me. I had saved up all my pocket money for weeks to buy something special. I had thought that today would be it; I could fit in with this group of girls and be a part of their gang. I remember that feeling of embarrassment of being the only one not getting a pair and pretending like I didn't care. But I really did. This felt like my only chance to be a part of this crew and I'd blown it because I was bigger than them.

I went home upset that evening and my mum must have called my nan Sybil, because a few days later she had hand-made me a pair using some fabric she had at home. The following week I went into town with those girls again and wore the trousers my nan had made me, thinking how cool it was that I had something the same as them. But their response wasn't what I'd hoped. The girls laughed when they discovered that they had been hand-made by my nan. They said they were cheap and the stitching wasn't as good as their branded pairs.

That was the last time I ended up hanging out with those girls.

In my head, I was obviously so fat that I didn't deserve clothes that were fashionable. I couldn't help but compare myself to others and find myself wanting. If I wanted to fit in, I would have to change myself to fit into those smaller numbers on the inside label of clothes.

How I found my confidence

I was lucky that I had my nan who would make me outfits and that was a huge distraction from the lack of wardrobe options for anyone above a UK size 14 (US 10) on the high street back then. She would cut, sew and embellish, and make me the most amazing and unique pieces.

Although the girls at school may have not liked my hand-made outfits, I did. I love my nan and she was the one who always surrounded me with love and kindness, and pushed the

'My nan always surrounded me with love and kindness.'

narrative that I should always unapologetically be myself.

Sybil and I would go to the local car boot sales and find the most outrageous seventies fabrics and eighties sequin blazers. Back then, going into charity shops wasn't quite the trendy phenomenon of 'vintage shopping' or 'thrift shopping' that it is today; it was seen as a sign you were poor and couldn't afford the high-street items. You would get bullied at school for wearing secondhand clothes. But the high street was never for me: not for my curves and, alas, not for my wallet.

I adore my nan and to me she is the most stylish person in the world. The way she puts together a bold, bright, eighties raspberry suit jacket with an emerald green turtleneck and a gold and pearl vintage brooch, matched with her perfect silver perm and coral lipstick – she looks incredible in these 'secondhand clothes'. She's always been the queen of fashion in my eyes. There's nothing negative about finding your own style with what is available to you, I actually praise this very much.

> ## 'Find your style with what is available to you.'

To be so-called 'fashionable', you have to have style. Style is not something that can be bought; it's something that grows organically from what you are surrounded and influenced by.

Dressing to stand out became my identity – I was 'the one who dressed weird' in my hometown. But I was already made to feel different because of my body shape, so I decided to take that label and make it my own.

How comparison culture leads to messed-up sizing

The journey from negative comparison to self-love and finding your own style is hard. As I say, I was lucky to have my nan help me find my way. But comparing yourself to others can have a huge effect on your confidence and can start to play on your mental health without you even realizing it. And the negative pressures come not only from your peers and the world around you, but even from the clothing manufacturers themselves.

Allow me to introduce you to one of my bugbears: that all of us, no matter what size we are, have to deal with the emotional trauma of being different sizes in different clothing stores. As a curvier woman I have always struggled to find styles that are equal to my smaller counterparts, but to add to this, every person I know, big or small, has had bruising encounters with the inconsistent and confusing sizing policies of different manufacturers around the globe.

Let's face it, we all have a bit of an emotional and warped relationship with sizing. Clothing brands know this, and there's no better way to make money than through messing with everyone's insecurities.

Vanity sizing dilemma

I should give credit where it's due to some clothing manufacturers: we do now have plus-size ranges on the high street so there has been some progress. But as is so often the case, it's one step forward and two steps back. And one of those backwards steps is something called vanity sizing, which is when certain brands deliberately manipulate their sizing to appear more desirable, but it's not always quite what you think. Let me elaborate.

Let's say you are the UK's current average clothing size, which is a size 16 (US size 12). You have struggled with finding your size in most shops like many of us and you constantly feel that the problem might in fact be you and the potential extra weight you've put on recently. Yet the chances are it has nothing to do with you and your body, it's the stores that are trying to convince you that buying their item with a different label to normal is the answer to your potential insecurities.

Imagine the scenario. You go out to buy a pair of jeans on the high street, and in the three stores below you fit the following sizes:

Shop no 1: You are a UK size 18 (US size 14) here.
Shop no 2: You are a UK size 14 (US size 10) here.
Shop no 3: You are a UK size 16 (US size 12) here.

Without hesitation, which shop do you think you would prefer to buy the jeans from? (This is your book and no one is listening so be honest with yourself.)

Chances are you have picked the store where you can fit into the UK size 14 (US size 10), and, if you have, I understand why. The issue here though, is *why* do we want to appear smaller? The fashion industry is pushing the narrative that being smaller is more desirable. They are treating us like spoiled children telling us what we want to hear, but in reality they are reinforcing the toxic message that big equals bad.

> **'Companies are allowing their fashions to be accessible only to those they want to cater for.'**

The problem is, the UK size 14 is not a size 14, it's actually a 16 and this is called vanity sizing. The company has made its clothes bigger and hasn't increased the jeans size to correspond, knowing you will spend your money where you appear to be a size smaller. Can you see how messed up this is?

You could have a size 109-cm (43-in) hip and be a UK 14 (US 10) in one store and a UK 16 (US 12) in another.

We then have the opposite end of the spectrum where brands are making their sizes smaller to cater only for a specific size range. You'll find this where they stock XS–L but the large is only a UK size 12/14 (US size 8/10). Not only does this confuse customers but it also alienates the majority of the public. To put this into context, the average woman in the UK is a size 16 (US size 12) and the average woman in the US is a size 14 (UK size 18). The situation where I have tried on a size large and the item of clothing has not even made it over my knees as it is so small has happened more times than I can remember. These companies are allowing their fashions to be accessible only to those they want to cater for. And in particular, this happens a lot with high-end designer houses.

Hidden fashion

While we're on the subject, I want to let you know that many of these high-end designers do cater to curves, but a lot of them don't have the items on display in their showrooms. Working as a model I've noticed this on set. Why is it that I've never been able to find a dress in my size in this designer's store, but suddenly it's available to a stylist for a big fashion publication? You are being sold a dream that you cannot be a part of unless you are a specific number on a size label or unless you are part of an unrealistic situation like a photoshoot. Sometimes being a model is just being a part of that fantasy.

> **'You are being sold a dream that you cannot be part of unless you are a specific number on a label.'**

The same thing occurs when we have a fuller-figured celebrity or musician walk or perform at a designer fashion show. We all jump for joy that they have been styled in the kind

of outfit we've always dreamed of buying, then we realize our size has not been made in the ready-to-wear collections. It turns out that piece was in fact a one-off for that person, because they are famous – and the rest of us better go look on the high street for knock-offs in the usual dizzying array of sizes, either sized smaller for brand aesthetic or sized bigger for vanity sizing to patronize us and make us feel like we might have a seat at the table soon.

There is a way to solve this, but these companies seem to be enjoying this yo-yo sizing experiment they are carrying out on all of us. What I also find rather crazy is that not only does this make shopping more difficult for us and play with our emotions, but it causes an insane amount of returns and packaging that could have been saved from landfill if we didn't have so many bizarre and inconsistent size charts.

> ## 'We need an industry standard across the whole nation.'

I truly believe if we had an industry standard across the whole nation it would help to tackle the emotional triggers, eating disorders and anxiety that sizing issues contribute towards, not to mention reducing the amount of waste it is inevitably causing for our planet.

What I find interesting is that there doesn't seem to be the same kind of issue when it comes to footwear. Vanity sizing just doesn't exist there. There are recognized industry standards in the UK, US, Europe, Australia, New Zealand – and all over the world. There are women's, men's and children's sizes and wide foot options, too, but the important thing is that the measurements are standard across the UK, EU and USA, just in different metrics. I don't often hear young people battle over the shoe size because the sizes are nationally stocked pretty equally, and the sizing doesn't change in different stores. Shopping for footwear is a walk in the park compared to shopping for clothes! So it proves that clothes manufacturers could also standardize their sizing, if they put their minds to it.

That said, I'm also aware that we do come in different heights and shapes as well as sizes, so certain styles might fit certain figures more than others. For example, if we looked at two women, both the same size, but different heights, a pair of dungarees might fit the taller lady better, due to the length of the fabric, their height, the material thickness and their curves etc. I'm not saying an industry standard sizing chart will mean you will fit into every style of clothing in your size. We will always have problems due to certain patterns, materials and styles, but imagine if we could just say, okay, this store caters for me and I will definitely find something in my size in a style that works for me. We would be able to avoid the stores that don't cater for us, as the industry standard would equalize the measurements and show the brands that really only stock up to a UK size 12 (US size 8). Hopefully this might be a wake-up call to them that they should increase their sizing and stop living in the past.

It blows my mind that the government doesn't enforce this. It would help so many.

It would also be great if there was a global industry standard, but with the different systems in each country I am not sure we would ever be able to get there.

International comparisons

Let's look at how they do things differently in other countries.

The sizing between the US and the UK is different. Looking at an international sizing chart as a British woman, you appear to go down two sizes if buying American clothing, as the US uses a different system to us. By the same token, if an American woman were to buy clothes in the UK, they would have to go up two sizes.

I've heard so many British women joke about 'not going on a diet for my holiday' if they're going to America because they will drop two sizes once they arrive in the country anyway. The problem is you haven't lost weight while travelling across the pond, you are just using a different country's sizing chart. You are not bigger or smaller in either country, it's just a different label. It's a shame that I've heard so many women use this fact to suggest they are better if they are a smaller size. Why promote the idea that being smaller is more desirable?

> **'Why promote the idea that being smaller is more desirable?'**

In South Korea, 'Free-Size' is their universal size, which is essentially one size fits all. The sizing comparison to this is a UK 6–8 or a USA 2–4. I cannot imagine the body dysmorphia that this must be causing its citizens. Although South Korea has one of the lowest obesity rates in the world, is it a coincidence that it has one of the world's highest rates of plastic surgery with an estimated one in three women going under the knife at least once in their lifetime, combined with the fourth-highest suicide rate for women in the world?

Body image issues are a global problem and we need to look into how we can disrupt those controlling ideals and find an inner peace by owning who we are, just how we want to be. Weight is not always the way to define someone's health, but being larger in society in this day and age is seen as the worst thing you can be. This is a narrative we need to change.

Not everyone who is fat is unhealthy and not everyone who is thin is healthy. It is all personal to that specific human. It's useless to compare yourself to others.

> **'Not everyone who is fat is unhealthy and not everyone who is thin is healthy.'**

When it comes to health it is very much a taboo subject to talk about how you can be body positive, overweight and healthy all at the same time.

How useful is BMI?

While we're on the subject of health and weight, I would like to talk about another way in which we are often encouraged to compare our bodies to others, and that is the BMI (body mass index) method of assessing your weight. In my opinion this is an outdated way to measure health based on the numbers on a scale. Did you know it was created in the 1830s? Why is it still being used today?

For those who don't know, to work out your BMI you do a simple calculation based on your height, weight, age and gender and you are then told your BMI. Here is the wording of the five categories in which you would be placed in the UK:

1. **Underweight**
2. **Healthy Weight**
3. **Overweight**
4. **Obese**
5. **Morbidly Obese**

The first issue I have is that there is no 'morbidly' underweight here. The focus is just that bigger is the worst outcome, and the biggest is the only morbid version.

I remember going to the doctor when I was young. I was around a UK size 14 (US size 10) at the time and I was told I was obese. I was smaller than the national average at that time but classed as obese. I had no health conditions but being told I was obese alienated me into thinking I should maybe start dieting. Luckily, I didn't take it to heart, but this is where an eating disorder could so easily have developed.

Some BMI examples

I want to put this to you:

- **Arnold Schwarzenegger**, poster boy of body building, is **OBESE** on the BMI scale.

- **Dwayne Johnson**, also known as 'The Rock', a retired wrestler now actor, is classed as **OBESE** on the BMI scale.

- **Amanda Bingson**, track and field athlete who has broken world Olympic records, is classed as **OBESE** on the BMI scale.

- **Gia Carangi**, known as the first-ever supermodel, was classed as a **HEALTHY WEIGHT** on the BMI scale, but in fact was struggling with mental health issues and severe drug abuse, which ultimately contributed to her death.

- Hollywood actor **Tom Cruise** is classed **OVERWEIGHT** on the BMI scale because of his 5'7" height.

- **Tony Romo**, quarterback for the Dallas Cowboys American football team, is classed as **MORBIDLY OBESE** on the BMI scale.

Do you think you can really define someone's health by what category they are classed on this scale? Some of these examples are literally playing sports and representing their country and are at the top of their game. I think you get the point I'm trying to make here. I'm also not saying every single people person who will be on the obese scale is healthy, but it's not equal across the board in either direction.

How did BMI start?

The scale surfaced in the 1830s when a Belgian statistician called Adolphe Quetelet developed a simple math formula after he became interested in the idea of plotting 'average' measurements of the human body on a graph.

The idea was taken up by insurance companies after home weighing scales began to be popular in the mid-20th century. For the first time, scales were being used by normal working people, not just professionals. With these measurements now regularly available, insurance companies started to gather data on their customers, believing that the more you weigh, the more chance you have of becoming sick and ultimately passing away at a younger age.

By the 1940s it was no surprise that an insurance company called Metropolitan Life had created its own standardized tables

based on its own version of the Quetelet scale, identifying what was deemed to be the desirable weight for its customers. Fast forward to today and BMI is still used for life insurance plans and, you guessed it, if you have a higher BMI your price will be affected.

Is this one of the reasons a better standard of defining health and weight hasn't yet been adopted, because so much money is riding on this outdated method, particularly in terms of how much we pay for our life insurance policies?

Food for thought.

Gender comparison in body positivity

Of course, comparison culture is not something that is limited to women – many men suffer from the same insecurities about their looks and weight. Fortunately, the male body positivity movement is finally starting to get momentum. There are so many incredible men who are now starting to open up about the things they have been conditioned to not speak about, including their bodies and their emotions.

However, although there has been some great work that's being done on that side, it's clear that the societal roles that are still present in the media mean that women are still generally getting the raw deal in terms of how their bodies are perceived.

Let's look at some recent representations of larger men and women on the cover of various fashion magazines, for example:

- **Rick Ross** on the cover of *Rolling Stone*
- **Melissa McCarthy** on the cover of *Elle*
- **James Cordon** on the cover of *GQ*
- **Gabby Sidibe** on the cover of *V Magazine*

The questions I put to you are:

- Which of these people are going to be praised solely for their talent?
- Which of these people are going to be seen as powerful because of their size?
- Which person's weight is going to be scrutinized?
- Which person's health is going to be mentioned first?

We all know that the answers to the first two questions will be the male celebrities, and the answers to the last two will be the female celebrities.

Every single curvier woman on the cover of a magazine will be targeted with questions about her weight, diet, exercise routine and personal life. I'm not saying all magazines do this – we have seen such a progression with female-run publications now – but even if they are being supported by the magazines, the scrutiny they get from the other tabloids, gossip websites and social media still exists. The ignorance surrounding weight and health is still rife, but why is it so often targeted at women? When you see a plus-size male figure on the cover of a magazine no one is talking about his weight in a negative manner; he is seen as a strong force who everyone loves because of his personality. James Corden, for example, is just known as the funny and loveable dude from all those American chat shows; his weight often gets ignored because of his presence, his larger-than-life laugh and joyous wit. But throw a woman into the mix and media is quick to pull her apart even if her personality is absolutely next level. That is why we need to keep working on female/non-binary/trans empowerment until we can be seen as equal counterparts to cisgender men.

The power of diversity

For so long, the fashion, music, press and entertainment industries have been run by men; men with ridiculous, outdated beauty ideals that, for so long, have favoured their fantasies of the tall, slender, white woman. We only have to look at Victoria's Secret when one of the senior execs said in 2018 that there was no place for trans or plus-size women at their shows. One of his poor excuses was that they had previously attempted to do a television special for plus-sizes and: 'No one had any interest in it. Still don't.'

The irony was that he then had to resign from the company as the internet did its thing to correct him for his misogynistic, sexist, sizeist and transphobic remarks. But for my own satisfaction, let's just read his statement again: 'No one had any interest in [plus-size]. Still don't.' Well, sorry to tell you, babes, but the plus-size market is now worth £128 billion ($178 billion) worldwide. Yes, that's right: £128 *billion*.

> **'The plus-size market is now worth £128 billion ($178 billion) worldwide.'**

In 2020, with a total revamp and new casting strategy in place, Victoria's Secret introduced their first openly transgender model Valentina Sampaio as one of their angels. They have been more diverse in their campaigns with more women of colour featured, and they have also used plus-size and older women.

Some might say this diversity announcement is too little too late for this company and they are simply trying to pick up the pieces from the mess their past employee made, but I hope his mistakes made others see the power we can have when we use our voices and stand up for diversity.

Speaking of someone who is doing diversity right, in catapults Rihanna with Savage X Fenty owning Fashion Week authentically back in 2017 and every single damn time since. Showcasing diversity in skin tone, ability, gender and size so effortlessly, but yet so powerfully. She showed everyone how it can be done.

> **'Imagine how powerful we would feel without constant comparison?'**

It's extraordinary to me that more companies haven't seen the benefits of this approach. Don't people understand the magnitude of power there is to be found in diversity? Not only for the pure fact representation should always be promoted, but also because the plus-size industry itself, as I mentioned above, is worth literally billions globally.

So why are brands still not expanding their sizes and gaining profit? They have been doing it for decades when it comes to beauty, fad diets and surgery, after all. Maybe it's because they understand the power of fashion – that if everything was easily available to us, if everyone catered for bigger sizes, our collective body confidence would skyrocket and less money would be spent trying to fit in with everyone else.

'Wear the cloak of confidence (available in all sizes).'

If I could have found a leopard-print catsuit, a baby pink leather jacket and a figure-hugging bikini that moulded to my curves as a teen, it would have been over for you all.

Jokes aside, imagine the strength we would have had earlier in our lives, had we been given that cloak of confidence (*available in all sizes*) when we were younger? Imagine feeling equal to our peers when going into the popular high-street store with our girlfriends on a Saturday and being able to buy the same items? Imagine not having to go into the older style stores with our parents as a teen and having to wear clothes aimed at middle-aged women, but actually being able to all rock the same look in a variety of sizing and feeling that big girl gang energy? Imagine how much better our mental health and views on our body would have been if we had felt an equality within the fashion industry? Imagine how powerful we would and could feel without constant comparison?

Social media comparison

Social media is a whole other ball game when it comes to comparison culture. The reality is that the majority of things we see online have been altered.

In Norway a law has just passed decreeing that any person posting sponsored content must not post any modified photos without declaring what they have had done. This doesn't affect normal photographs being edited, just ones that are paid partnerships. The people who have these paid contracts are the likes of models, influencers, actors and musicians – in other words, the people who are popular and admired, with high follower counts. Now if there is a tag openly showing that all these really aspirational and unattainable photos have been altered, I think it would help to counteract people's negative body image issues. Sometimes people are so absorbed in other people's fantasies, they need to be labelled to be clear that they are not real. It is an illusion.

> **'The majority of things we see online have been altered.'**

I personally think this is brilliant and I hope other countries, including the UK and US, catch on. After all, if you were to add extra additives to a food product to make it sweeter, you would have to label this information on the packaging when you are selling it, otherwise it is false advertising and could be harmful

Comparison reminders

When you are looking at someone's 'perfect' life online and feeling like you don't add up, remember these important points:

1. Instagram is essentially a visual CV where the majority are posting their very best experiences as a highlight reel.

2. A lot of people use photo-editing apps such as Facetune so nothing is exactly what it seems.

   The people you believe have the perfect life – the celebrities, the bloggers and the influencers – are probably feeling the pressure from society to continue this narrative.

3. If you aren't on their close friends story, you probably aren't getting the full version of themselves.

4. Take control. Ultimately, if someone makes you question yourself, feel insecure or has a negative effect on your self-esteem, unfollow them. Unfollow people online as you would stop hanging out with them in real life if they made you feel bad.

to the consumer. This is essentially what this new law in Norway is ensuring and I think it is a step in the right direction to reduce body pressures and the detrimental impact they have on people.

It's ultimately about being transparent in what you have edited or manipulated, which I think is important when you are in a position of influence and you are selling things to your audience.

In fact, I'd go further: in my opinion, selling a beauty product but using editing apps that change your face and appearance, is tantamount to body image fraud.

How to harness comparison for good: vision boards

One thing that personally helps me dig deeper into who I am, what I want and how I would like to grow is creating something known as 'vision boards'. These are basically scrapbooks of thoughts, feelings, inspirations and images that make you feel good and will help you align with your future aspirations.

The only comparison you have here is with the person you are now and the person you want to become.

> **'Manifest the journey of your future.'**

Vision boards are a product of your own mindset and thoughts, not what others have imposed on you. The aim is to help you discover your true values and what you want in life, rather than the shallow desires that are simply reflections of what you've digested online. They will help you focus on different areas of your life and manifest the journey of your future – whether that's the growth of love, the trajectory of your career or the timeline for achieving your dreams.

I usually do this at the start of a year, but you could also do it before your next birthday or simply start at a random time that suits you, with no particular milestone in mind.

No two vision boards are the same – and yours will be as unique as you are – but here is an example of what I use to make mine, to give you some inspiration and help you get started. You will need:

- **Large piece of card** (I often go for a bright colour)
- **Marker pens** – lots of colours
- **Tape** – I use masking tape so I can write on top of it
- **Bright stickers** – to make it look eye-catching and fun
- **Photographs or magazine cuttings** – for inspiration

Start out by dividing your card into four sections. I use the following categories, but these should be completely personal to you and your aspirations:

1. Career
2. Relationships
3. Travel
4. Home

In each section, write down what you would like to achieve, for example:

1. What career goal would you like to achieve in the next year?
2. How would you like to see your relationships with friends, family and/or your partner blossom over the next year? Are there any specific milestones you want to achieve?
3. Where would you like to travel and what would you like to explore?
4. Where would you like to live, who with and how would you decorate your space?

Next, get creative and have some fun with it – add stickers, words of affirmation, photographs and anything else to decorate your vision board to reflect your personality.

The power of manifestation

The idea behind manifestation is simple. A popular online definition is: 'Manifestation is the theory that through regular meditation and positive, constructive thought, you can make your dreams and desires become reality.'

'Comparison is the swindler of happiness.'

Even if you don't believe in this, the power of putting positive thoughts out there for your future is only a good thing and once you start to see those things happen a week, a month or a year down the line, the contentment you will feel knowing you processed those thoughts is pretty special.

Vision boards are very much part of this process. You can either display your vision board in your home, or like me you can hide it under your bed, going back to look at it in a month or maybe even a year later to see what has changed.

You may not have landed that dream job you wanted, but maybe instead you have worked hard at getting the right experience under your belt, which will help your career travel in the right direction. It's not always the biggest thing on your vision board that makes the change, sometimes it's the smallest.

'Believe in your own hype.'

For example, on my vision board from last year, I wrote down that I wanted to front a campaign for the British nature-based beauty company, The Body Shop, as I love their ethics and everything they promote to the world. I also wanted to push my brand Self-Love Brings Beauty in a new direction with words of teaching and affirmation. I never did get that campaign, but I got asked to supply my Self-Love Mantras for the Body Shop's Self-Love Aid Kit packs. It was a dream come true and that came up from the roots of the vision board. It didn't just grow onto one branch, but grew into various leaves that fell into the right path.

The power of positive thoughts, manifestations and believing my own hype has been something that has really helped me stop comparing myself to others, their work ethic, their travel paths and relationships. Instead, it has made me look deep inside myself, be proud of the journey I have been on and excited about what the future holds.

I truly believe that comparison is the swindler of happiness. So let's write down all the amazing things you are going to put into fruition and let's not allow the harmful habit of comparison to take away your shine.

'I believe in the power of manifestation.'

A Place at the High-Fashion Table

I am very lucky that now in my career I have a great team of people behind me and with that I get invited to some of the best fashion events and parties, with one of the most prestigious occasions of the year in the UK being the British Fashion Awards.

I've been attending for a few years now and one of the reasons I feel it is important to go is because even though we have made *some* steady progress with size diversity in campaigns and editorial, we don't seem to be quite up there with it in the flesh in the UK in these events. We are still leading the way with the same high-end, 'sample size' fashion models being the faces of these bougie parties. I like to think my presence there, no matter how small, brings some body diversity and gives hope to others that these doors are being opened for us, no matter how slowly.

Sticking to my principles

In 2019, however, I stuck to my principles by declining my invite to the British Fashion Awards. Now, don't get me wrong, I love a bit of glitz and glam and a chance to prove my belief that bigger women deserve to be in these spaces too, but this year was different.

To attend the event you either need to be nominated or be invited by a brand. That year I was invited by a company who I then realized had only invited me to tick a box in their diversity quota and couldn't care less about making me feel comfortable.

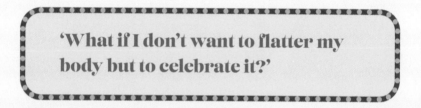

'What if I don't want to flatter my body but to celebrate it?'

You may think I am being overdramatic here, but it really is the bigger picture I was thinking about. When you are invited to these events by a brand, they will dress you; you are basically a walking advertisement for them. So there I was, going to the fitting for one of the most exciting fashion nights of the year and, once I'd arrived, I was led to the showroom to pick my outfit. There were two other attendees there, both smaller industry sizes and both had a whole rail of outfits to choose from. As for me, however, I was taken to my 'section' that had one item hanging up waiting for me. One oversized cape-style dress that wasn't even my correct size, but would fit because it was the size of a two-man tent. My counterparts had ten or twelve options and I was made to feel like I should be grateful for what I was offered.

Embarrassed, I pretended to like the dress and left the showroom, but it then began to grate on me. Solely because of my size, I had been given the booby-prize option. Plus-size women are often an afterthought when it comes to fashion, to sizing and to style. We are often made to feel like we should hide our figures or wear items that are deemed 'flattering'. What if I don't want to flatter my body but to celebrate it? I'm not going to be made to feel grateful for one dress option. I'm not going to attend the awards and give your brand free press, tick your diversity quota and feel like I'm about to set up a campfire and toast some marshmallows on the red carpet in my new oversize tent dress that you've so kindly offered to me. Thanks, but no thanks!

I sat at home, ordered a takeaway, put on *Girls Trip* and posted online:

 Felicity Hayward

I cancelled on going to the British Fashion Awards tonight because the brand taking me offered me one dress option, whereas everyone else who was a smaller size got the pick of the store. I might look like I'm being petty, but I'm not going to be made to feel grateful for the opportunity … when I am always an afterthought with these brands.

The post went viral and made various news outlets in a matter of hours. I got more of a positive reaction for not attending and sticking to my ethos, than I would have done by attending and not being authentically myself.

Sometimes you might feel like you are making a big mistake and letting others down if you turn something down, but if you truly know that it's out of your comfort level, let it pass by.

It's the bigger picture here. We don't just want tent-style dresses and we don't want to be an afterthought.

The same problem arose at London Fashion Week, too.

'We would love for Felicity to attend our show this season, but unfortunately we can't do dressing.' It's a carefully crafted email that has become the norm for me to receive prior to London Fashion Week and, quite honestly, I'm bored of it. I'm tired of supporting an industry that doesn't support me and women of my size – so in February 2020 I decided to boycott LFW. The previous season was so poor when it came to diversity and inclusion that I decided to give my energy to New York Fashion Week instead, hoping London would prove me wrong that season.

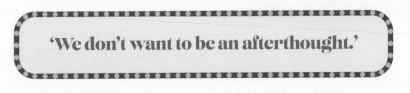

'We don't want to be an afterthought.'

One reason for this was because I would likely end up sitting front row at the shows, surrounded by other people dressed head to toe in that designer's clothes, and by contrast I would be lucky to be offered a pair of earrings or a handbag.

I used to be so grateful for this, but again, like the Fashion Awards, it's a double-edged sword: show up and be the diversity, or cancel and make a statement. The latter has

'It's not about one type of body or beauty ideal any more.'

suddenly become more appealing, not only for my brand ethos, but for my sanity. You wouldn't go to a dinner party where you were only allowed the basic lunch menu and everyone else is offered the three-course à la carte with wine pairings, would you? If you don't support plus-size, I'm not coming to give you free coverage, my time and my energy.

The thing is with London, I could probably count on one hand how many plus-size models I've seen walk shows here. I love London, I really do. I moved here when I was 17 to study and it was the place where I found my squad of friends who made me feel that being different is accepted here. London is also the place where so many iconic fashion labels and brands were born. London created punk and it remains a pioneer for a plethora of trends and talented designers. So why are we still so far behind when it comes to diversity both on the runway and with designers?

Plus-size model Ashley Graham recently spoke to American designer Christian Siriano (who shows at New York Fashion Week) in her podcast, Pretty Big Deal, about this very subject, asking him, 'Is it hard to cater for bigger sizes?' He replied, 'It takes time but my small team of 20 still seem to be able to do it, so I'm not sure why others can't.' To me, that spoke volumes.

So why are plus-size women not included; not seen at the shows? I think the answer goes much deeper than not being able to find the right dress.

Every season during the shows, I take my seat and pray I will see some sort of improvement in diversity. But every year, I'm disappointed: I'm lucky if I see one or two women walking at LFW who are even slightly curvy. London just doesn't take risks when it comes to body diversity – and it's starting to show.

After all, we live in a society where the rise of social media has influenced how people feel about fashion and identity. As an audience, we want to see something real; we want to be able to relate and it's not just about one type of body or beauty ideal any more.

Equality in beauty

What Rihanna has achieved with her Fenty fashion enterprise is a great example of this. You only have to see the look books of Fenty Beauty campaigns to realize that she is making her brands accessible to everyone.

I attended the Savage X Fenty show in New York in 2019 and I was literally in tears. There stood Bella Hadid, one of the world's most famous supermodels, next to a size 22 model dripping in lace and diamonds. A plus-size dancer and a model with a prosthetic leg then took to the stage. Every single one of those women glowed. They looked empowered and there was no hierarchy among them: they were all considered equal in their beauty.

That show did something to people. It showed love, respect and power. It portrayed a fierce human force that was an army to be reckoned with. This is how the world really looks now, and Rihanna reflected that in her fashion offerings.

As a British woman it infuriates me that we aren't seeing the equivalent of this in London. Is it because Britain doesn't have as many plus-size icons as they do in the States? Or is it simply that there's less pressure to dress curvier celebrities, so designers avoid the issue in shows, too?

Where is the British designer using a range of full-figured and slim, tall and short, young and old models? The brand that is representing all different backgrounds and skin tones, all sexualities and all genders? Why is the USA so much further ahead than the UK? Rihanna's Savage X Fenty was so successful it was bought by Amazon Prime and I can safely say one of the reasons it was so hugely popular was because so many people felt seen, felt represented, felt sexy, felt empowered and ultimately bought into her brand and line. Why wouldn't anyone want to have that level of sales and success over in the UK?

> **'That show did something to people. It showed love, respect and power.'**

In the 2020 London fashion season, we did actually see some plus-size representation, which of course I was thrilled to be wrong about … but it was minimal. One of the main things that left me quite frustrated was how one designer went about using curve models. Lena Dunham, creator and star of *Girls*, walked for an indie fashion brand and to no one's surprise gained a lot of press for them.

'She embodies what our brand stands for … Lena has fun with fashion,' said a spokesperson for the brand. That statement is true – Lena definitely does, and so do most of us curvier women when we have the opportunity to be included.

I was so excited that a London brand would now fit me, especially as Dunham, who I believe is around a UK size 18 (USA size 14), walked for them, but upon looking on their website I couldn't find any stock beyond a UK size 16 (US size 12), with the majority of their items only going up to a UK size 14 (US size 10). It's been well over a year since that show, so they have had the opportunity to extend their sizing, but they haven't. I've gone from thinking, 'Great, it's a step in the right direction,' to then thinking, 'Was this just plus-size tokenism with a celebrity again?'

At least with Roland Mouret and Tommy Hilfiger, who also had collections that season, both used curve models and they also had shoppable pieces on site. Don't give us a token slice of diversity if we can't actually be part of the crew.

> **'Don't give us a token slice of diversity if we can't actually be part of the crew.'**

Going back to New York designer Christian Siriano, this is his take on the subject, affirming his company's decision to design for women of all body types:

'It is simply bad business to ignore a demographic. We order most production runs of the Christian Siriano Collection up to US size 18 [or UK size 22], as that is what our retailers order from us. However, when any piece from our collection is desired in a size not pre-produced, we can make it custom for the client.'

This is from the designer who created Billy Porter's iconic Oscar tuxedo gown in 2019. Siriano also famously dressed 17 women for the Oscars in 2018, including Whoopi

Goldberg, Janelle Monáe, Amy Adams, Laverne Cox, Christina Hendricks and Keala Settle – each of whom exude their own style, size and beauty. Wouldn't it be nice if this wasn't seen as trailblazing, but normal?

An alternative approach

The energy, to me, feels very different at New York Fashion Week to London. Is this because the US has a much bigger population and their average size is a US size 14 (UK size 18), compared to a British average of UK size 16 (US size 12)? Or is it that Americans are just generally more forward-thinking and advanced in diversity than in the UK?

It's not just the shows that are more diverse; there are more events, opportunities and brands that include curves, making the US shine brightly as a beacon of inclusion.

You have photographers such as Brooklyn-based Lydia Hudgens, who is photographing solely plus-size street style for a large online platform. There are influencers like Kellie Brown, who is promoting the plus-size presence with her own hashtags and the movement AndIGetDressed. There's also writer Gianluca Russo, who is talking about the male plus-size movement and inclusivity for many media outlets.

There's none of this in my hometown of London. The only plus-size representation I ever seem to see at London Fashion Week is *Stylist* magazine's fashion features editor Billie Bhatia, and the occasional model or two.

New York has curve-specific events: the fashion brand 11 Honoré, for example, hosts private dinners with a range of top curve models and influencers. They are true celebrations of women and by no means a gimmick.

I can't begin to tell you how incredible it was to walk into the 11 Honoré showroom in New York and find a Dolce & Gabbana dress in my size. It was a wonderful and luxurious shopping experience. Could we do this in London? Did you even know Dolce & Gabbana has plus-size clothes? They actually became the first luxury heritage house to offer ready-to-wear pieces above a US size 16 (UK size 20) when it went up to US size 18 (UK size 22) in 2019.

Do you understand how ground-breaking that is? At the same time, do you understand how sad it actually is to say it's ground-breaking to find a designer in your size? Do you understand your privilege if this is something so regularly available to you? Do you understand the feeling of always feeling less than your smaller friends due to lack of availability in fashion?

It's not just Dolce that 11 Honoré stocks either; there's a beautiful showroom showcasing designers including Christopher Kane (up to a UK size 22/US size 18), Prabal Gurung (up to a UK size 24/US size 20), Sally Lapointe (up to a UK size 26/US size 22), Veronica Beard (up to a UK size 28/US size 24) and Christian Siriano (up to a UK size 28/US size 24).

Most of these designers also show at NYFW, meaning you can buy a designer piece in your size and attend the same designer's show wearing it. UNREAL.

In a recent season in New York, so many models were walking for these big designers: Precious Lee for Christian Siriano, Candice Huffine for Veronica Beard, Saffi Karina for Serena Williams, Paloma Essler for Eckhaus Latta and Alexis Ruby for Marc Jacobs. We also saw independent designers such as Rene' Tyler using models from UK sizes 18 to 28 (US sizes 14 to 24) including plus-size teen model Lex Gibbon.

'All types of bodies being represented should be the norm.'

The swim and bodywear brand Chromat also stole the show with its diverse presentation using models of all genders, abilities and sizes to once again prove how forward-thinking the brand is with its inclusion.

It's not just the US; Europe is also making great strides in representation. Let's hop over to Paris Fashion Week:

- **Tommy Hilfiger** – an abundance of plus-size women at the Zendaya collaboration show in 2019.
- **Chanel** – had the first plus-size model to walk for Chanel in over ten years (Autumn/Winter 2020).

And what about Milan Fashion Week, also for Autumn/Winter 2020?

- **Fendi** – two plus-size models walking for the first time.
- **Versace** – three plus-size models walking for the first time.

It's finally happening: the high-end fashion houses are taking note. I just don't get why the UK is so behind, especially given the figures: the plus-size market was estimated to be worth $24 billion in the US in 2020, and is estimated to rise to around £9 billion in the UK in 2022.

Isn't the money enough to make designers and brands open up to the opportunities inclusive sizing and representation will bring? Surely one of the top priorities in a business is to make money? Or is 'plus-size' deemed such a filthy word that brands still don't want to associate their clothes with bigger people?

The truth is, I am embarrassed that the UK isn't catering for plus-size women; I'm embarrassed that I'm having to research different countries to try to find places where curvier humans

are seen as equal. I'm embarrassed that currently my own country is so far behind when it comes to size diversity in fashion. I'm embarrassed that the rest of the fashion weeks globally are making changes that LFW should have taken onboard a long time ago. And I'm frustrated that we don't seem to want, or be trying, to catch up, when quite frankly all types of bodies being represented should be the norm.

But let's move on from all this. We've looked at some of the problems that the outside world has thrown at us in our journey to self-acceptance. Now let's look deep within ourselves and harness our own power so that we can change our relationship with our bodies going forward.

The Self-Love Manifesto

You have now digested all the information on the body positive industry, the toxic side to body image, social media and comparison culture. You have not only read about, but most probably have had, personal experience of the trials and tribulations of what we endure by simply existing in our own bodies, through the timelines of trends and toxic diet culture. So you can see why there is such a huge body image crisis, right? I think it's time we looked deep within ourselves to find an antidote to this toxicity by writing down our ideas, thoughts and feelings and turning them into mantras that we can commit ourselves to work on in our daily lives.

Self-love is something that took me many years to find and fully understand and is also something I am continuing to grow and develop. I do wish that I had written down all my inner reflections and assumptions on the world and my body earlier so I could look back on them now and see how much I have blossomed, and that is exactly why I want you to start here today.

Let's start OWNING our bodies; let's start a new chapter, a new page, a new mindset. Let's write our own Self-Love Manifesto.

'Let's start OWNING our bodies; let's start a new chapter ... let's write our own Self-Love Manifesto.'

I want this to be a space where you can write your personal goals, thoughts and aspirations. A space in which you can come back, track your growth or change the goalposts on a particular feeling that has now passed. You'll be so proud of yourself, babes. If you are having a little bit of a wobble, you can come back to these pages and read one of the mantras to give yourself a little pocket of power!

Don't worry: I am going to walk you through it and share my current Self-Love Manifesto with you as an example. Remember, this isn't a comparison contest; it's all subjective to you and your journey. My manifesto is simply here to guide you into creating your own bespoke version. There are no wrong answers here.

Self-Love Manifesto

Self-love to me is finding a ...

... moment to appreciate my body for being strong, resilient and for having my back (literally) and working on ways to make sure I show it kindness.

I will understand that ...

... the perfect body does not exist as there are no two humans on the planet that are the same, so I should aspire to be the best version of myself, not someone else.

I will ignore ...

... targeted diet ads and anyone promoting unrealistic beauty ideals online. I will block or unfollow anyone or any pages on social media that I believe to be toxic.

I believe that ...

... unlearning bad habits and patterns will take time and I must not be too hard on myself when I am trying the best I can.

Now it's your turn to fill in the gaps. As I said, there are no wrong answers; this is your journey.

Self-love to me is finding a ...

I will understand that ...

I will ignore ...

I believe that ...

I will wear ...

...more leopard print in my life as it makes me feel sexy.

I will think ...

... less about other people's perceptions of me based on my appearance.

I will choose ...

... someone who deserves to be around my energy.

My body has survived ...

... plenty of heartbreak, but each time I have come out with a valuable lesson of growth. I must always remember that.

I promise to ...

... not feel guilty about removing people in my life when I feel the energy is not equal.

I will wear ...

I will think ...

I will choose ...

My body has survived ...

I promise to ...

Creating Your Own Personal Brand

Developing your own unique style is something that doesn't happen overnight; it's a process that takes time and you need to start off on the right path. If there is one thing I want to address at the start of this chapter, it is that you should always stay true to your authentic self.

During this journey of finding your own style, you may come across people who try to pressure you into changing who you really are, whether these are friends, loved ones, people at school or colleagues at work, and you will also experience the influence of popular culture and the media. Although it might feel like that moment of transformation to suit others fills a void, that fulfilment won't last forever and you will have wished you had stayed with your true self. Trust me on that one.

The power of authenticity

You now know about my journey, my struggles being at the front of the line in the plus-size modelling world when there weren't many options for us, especially jobs. I was thrown in at the deep end with no previous knowledge on how to act, what to wear, or any sort of fashion rules. I would turn up to castings wearing catsuits, eyeliner and platforms, quickly realizing that the girl-next-door look was the way you were supposed to turn up to meet potential casting directors. You were meant to arrive as a plain version of yourself ready to be used as a ragdoll for fashion.

Around that time at the start of my career, the only other curvy models I knew were girls who were pretty and wholesome-looking, and who wore quite plain clothing. They had thick thighs but flat stomachs and often wore padding to castings and jobs.

Padding is shaped foam pads, that look similar to 1980s' shoulder pads that are worn under knickers to enhance a women's hips, bum and legs. You can imagine my face when I realized pretty much every girl sitting in the casting room was heading to the bathroom to add these in before being seen by the casting director, and there I was looking down at my thighs thinking, 'Oh dear, babes, I can't take you off when I get home. It's me and you forever, baby.'

It was around 2014–2015 at this point. All the commercial jobs were booking those type of girls and I did wonder to myself, do I need to change? Do I need to go back to my natural mousey brown hair; do I need to tone down my fashion sense to try to fit in a little more? Do I need to lose weight so I can achieve the same body as the girls with padding in, even though that is not their real shape?

Perhaps if I did all that I would be able to pay my rent on time and prove to my parents this wasn't another one of my phases I was going through and this really was my full-time job?

Thankfully I am a stubborn Leo Sun, Leo Rising and Aries Moon woman (triple fire I know, lol) and I didn't change. I knew deep down I would be unhappy if I did and the voice of my nan would tell me to stick to my own identity and if they didn't like it, they could lump it!

'Never change for anyone.'

Fast-forward to now and I'm incredibly grateful that my career blossomed from not just being a model but also to being an inclusive lingerie designer, presenter and business owner with Self-Love Brings Beauty. It has also given me the opportunity to write this book, something that has always been on my vision board (see page 109–11). None of this would have happened if I had changed myself back then to fit into a mould.

Being authentic and sticking to my brand benefited me in the end, but it took time. I want you to listen to your intuition and your passion. Never change for anyone. You need to be authentically yourself, because one day we will win this battle against fat phobia, against body image orthodoxy, and you will be so happy you stuck to your guns and didn't follow the showbiz sheep; you didn't try to look like the padded crew; and you stayed true to what your gut told you.

Find your passion

I often get asked by others on how to get into the industry, how to become a model or content creator and I always tell them: find out the things you like about yourself and explore them. Create a social media page where you don't just show fashion and modelling, but also your hobbies, aspirations and influences. Be a rounded person, not just a clothes horse.

> **'Find out the things you like about yourself and explore them.'**

Over the past decade within the modelling industry, brands have started to change how they cast for their latest campaigns. They don't just want regular models any more, they want people with a passion, a story and things they believe in. You see this in other industries, too, where companies are slowly starting to see the value in the whole person rather than just viewing them as one-dimensional employees. I find this so refreshing. It proves that you can and should be more than just your title, your description or your grades on paper. You can have a voice and express yourself in ways that were often hidden before. I have seen the fashion industry change from models and bloggers being the only two types of creatives online, to models becoming influencers and bloggers becoming models. It's all come full circle. I truly believe the move towards realness has moulded the industry into something much more attainable, personable and relatable. It gives accessibility to people who don't feel like they fit in. It allows us to search online and find people who relate to our values and aesthetics. It opens up space for more people to join in. Of course that doesn't mean to say that we've attained equal representation across the board – there are still limitations if you're disabled, gender non-conforming, or minority-ethnic. There's clearly still a long way to go before things are truly inclusive but it is slowly opening up.

We are only on this planet for a short amount of time and you should make sure that there is always a happiness to fall back on, whether that happiness is a person, a place, a hobby or a small business you might decide to push further in the future. Everything we do in life is temporary, everything changes. Be prepared for that change by making sure you have things around you that authentically bring you joy when the wind suddenly turns in a different direction.

Just as you will have done in your vision board, write down the things you want to explore in the future because those thoughts, processes and ideas could blossom into something that could make you change direction on your journey.

How to find your own style

Okay, so let's start your style transformation by looking at where you spend your hard-earned money. One of the key pieces of advice I have when it comes to finding your own brand, style and true self is to urge you to support those fashion houses or those brands who do cater to you, your size, your ethos and your message.

Don't support someone who will only provide you with a belt or an earring in their store; don't line the pockets of people who don't appreciate you. Instead find the small independent brands who cater to the plus-size market. Support the companies who are not editing out stretch marks, scars, acne, cellulite and hair loss. Support the ones who are trying their best to represent you.

On the opposite page you will find a list of my current favourite brands (both in the UK and US) who have made a conscious effort to be size-inclusive or who are currently working on increasing their size ranges. The brands range from high street, designer and independent to sustainable, eco and fast fashion. I make no apologies for including fast fashion: unfortunately most sustainable extended-size brands are priced at a point that only the privileged can afford. I hope eventually the message will get through that eco labels can be for all sizes, because right now we are still fighting to get equal fashion options from the mainstream brands.

Alder Apparel

Alice Alexander

Anthropologie Plus

ASOS

Benjamin Fox

Birdsong

Boohoo

Carolina Herrera

Christian Siriano

Christopher Kane

Chromat

Collusion

Elena Mirò

Erdem

Girlfriend Collective

H&M+

Henning

Kai Collective

Karen Millen Curve

Kirrin Finch

Lane Bryant

Lapointe

Levi's

Loud Bodies

Mango Violeta

Mara Hoffman

Marina Rinaldi

Mary Benson

Monki

Nasty Gal

Never Fully Dressed

Playful Promises

Plus Equals

Pretty Little Thing

Rebdolls

Reformation Extended

River Island Plus

Savage X Fenty

Simply Be

Torrid

Universal Standard

Veronica Beard

... And, of course, Self-Love Brings Beauty (got to bring a little love for my own brand here!)

If we all do our bit to support the companies that are making an effort to be more inclusive, then perhaps it will help other companies to make a change. That said, where you buy your clothes is only half the battle. It's how you wear them that counts ...

'Dress for your body shape, not the number on a garment label.'

How to find your confidence with style

I believe the most stylish thing you can ever wear is confidence and the key to finding that confidence is comfort.

In order for me to feel my full sassy self I need to make sure the items I wear actually sit on my body in a way that make me feel cosy. I need to feel comfortable and for years I really didn't. I tried to morph my body into maintaining one dress size and as mentioned before we know that the dress sizes are insanely different in every store.

The one thing I want to say is forget the size labels: national and international sizing charts are a myth (see page 95–6). They are all different for every brand or fashion house so if you try to squeeze, tuck, zip up and squish your body into a certain size or shape that doesn't fit you purely due to the measurements on the label, we are going to have problems.

> 'The most stylish thing you can ever wear is confidence.'

I would start my personal style makeover by having a big wardrobe organize, or in my eyes my very own catwalk show. Blast your favourite disco tunes and start getting out all the pieces from your closets and trying every item of clothing on. Make a pile of pieces that make you feel good and make another pile to be donated, sold or given away. Sometimes we hold onto pieces that we may longer fit into, either because we've got bigger or smaller, and sometimes it's time to let them go. If they are making you feel less than because you have changed size or shape then it's time to let go of those memories. We evolve, change and grow as humans and it might be time for a big wardrobe detox and cleanse. The items that no longer fit you could be recycled and given to a new home, where they could turn into someone else's cloak of confidence.

Now, look at your favourite piece of clothing and ask yourself: why does it make you feel good? Is it the print, is it the colour, the texture, the shape, the length, or is it just simply a gut feeling?

My favourite item of clothing is

I love it because

For example, let's say your favourite piece is a wrap summer dress, which fits perfectly to your curves. It's that one staple that you know makes you feel like Beyoncé walking down the street, even if it's pouring with rain and you're late for work.

Now perhaps there is no opportunity to buy another version of this mood-enhancing dress due to the price point, or the item is out of stock. Or maybe you got this in a vintage shop, or a fashion store that no longer exists. Don't let that put you off. Get creative: go look for some vintage fabrics in thrift shops, or go to your local fabric shop or weekly street market. Find a print that fits with your aesthetic, a colour that fits in with your personality or a texture that suits your vibe.

> **'Fashion doesn't have to be expensive; it should be about having fun and expressing yourself.'**

Next go online, find a local seamstress or fashion student, or ask a friend or family member who you know is good at dressmaking to see if they can make your own version of your favourite dress. We don't just have to rely on the high street; you can get creative yourself. This also might be a nice activity to do with friends. You could all find the same fabric and make something for each other using the same material, going back to that biker girl gang aesthetic again (see page 106). If brands don't wanna cater for all of us, at all of our sizes, let's make our own home-made uniform that represents us!

I can see my gang doing this with a leopard-print fabric – one making a headband, one making a headscarf, one making a wraparound skirt and one making patches for jackets. The possibilities are endless! Fashion doesn't have to be expensive, it should be about having fun and expressing yourself.

Let's go back to your wardrobe. Maybe you have found your favourite black jersey dress, the one that is super comfy and fits your body perfectly, the one that can be worn casually when doing your weekly food shop, and the one that you can always wear out for dinner but that doesn't feel too 'dressy'. The one that when you might be having a difficult body-image day, or you are tired, restless and wanting to wear something you feel safe in, you can throw on for ease.

I say comfort is key so build on top of this piece with layers of fun to bring out your personality and style that might be hidden on that day. For example, get out all your accessories – necklaces, statement earrings, scarves, faux fur collars and colourful handbags. Adding a colour or texture to a simple dress can instantly sass up your look and bring it from day to night. Adding a colourful fun heel or platform and wearing a bold colour eyeshadow can instantly lift the look.

Once you've played around with these items you can see how easy it is to jazz up any item you have in your wardrobe; it's all about experimenting with what you have at home, playing with colours that bring you happiness and contentment.

Don't dress for anyone else's idea of what suits your body shape

Now let's talk body shape. Although I want you to know that you are in fact a tasty snack, I also want you to ignore the people who tell you your body is an apple, pear, pineapple or whatever other ridiculous fruits they like to describe you as, in order to influence you into an awful peplum skirt or vertical-line dress to change your appearance. You don't have to be a certain shape to wear what is considered 'flattering' to your shape. You also don't have to make yourself appear smaller in order to be deemed more beautiful. Flattering to me makes me feel like we are saying our bodies only look good when they appear to be smaller or hidden. We are all different and how we choose to show our bodies is our own choice. I personally love to wear tight figure-hugging catsuits, because:

1. **They are super comfy.**
2. **They make me feel like a boss bitch.**
3. **I feel sexy in them.**

To another woman, a beautiful oversize summer dress will make her feel like the most gorgeous version of herself and that's cool, too. Another person could feel comfortable in a colour-pop tailored suit. It's all about personal preference. It's all about listening to your body and what you physically and mentally feel good in. I love to explore charity/thrift shops; these are the places where there are a variety of sizes, shapes and clothing from all eras. They give you a chance to explore things that you might not see in the high street and explore your own style; they don't have vanity sizing; they aren't aimed at any one type or fashion ego or trend; they are humble, eco-friendly, treasure-trove, garment shops where you could find a diamond in the rough!

I truly believe that once you've found comfort within your style and wardrobe, your outer confidence and shine will start to blossom into the hydrangea flower garden of dreams it should always have been. It's all about taking it back to basics and building up those layers around you. And that doesn't just

What's going on underneath?

There is one thing that I do believe we should listen to when it comes to measurements and that is underwear. A good bra can be your biggest support during the day and it's so important if you are choosing lingerie to make sure that you have the correct fitted bra! Again, comfort is key with this one, and once you have found the correct size, other items of clothing will start to sit better on your silhouette. There are also now so many incredible brands who are catering for the busty babes of the world as well as the plus-size crew. We are now seeing brands such as Playful Promises (with whom I have my own lingerie line) and Savage X Fenty cater to a wide range of sizing that keeps expanding each season, so if you've got boobies and want to wear a bra, get those beauties measured – apparently 80 per cent of us are wearing the wrong size!

reflect on what we are talking about here with your wardrobe and style, but it also relates to your mind, thoughts, aspirations and influences.

> # 'How we choose to show our bodies is our own choice.'

Once we allow ourselves to dig deep …

- into the root cause of why we are anxious about our bodies
- into why social media plays such a huge part on the state of our mental health
- into why the high street seems to cater only for certain sizes – or manipulates us into thinking numbers on a label are the most important thing to look out for
- into all the toxic influences that are shoved into our faces daily
- into how we can take the power back and remove anything that no longer serves us
- into what truly makes us happy as individuals, what gives us that warm fuzzy feeling inside, what brings us excitement and joy

… that is when our style will overpower the outside influences and we can work on ourselves at our own pace, and that is when our true, authentic self will bloom.

Taking Care
of You

Self-care is important because when you are running on empty it affects not only your physical health but your mental health.

When you are feeling low, not only can you not achieve your best for yourself, but you also can't be the best for other people around you, whether that be in the workplace, in a relationship or in a friendship.

We often praise people who are 'booked and busy' but we all know you can't achieve everything you're capable of without recharging yourself, too. The goal really should be to be booked, not busy and having time to rest.

I believe self-care and body positivity are linked. When you are looking after yourself properly, you can truly be more content with who you are and what you have around you. Finding comfort in the simplest of things can bring a calmness into your realm. Sometimes a little endorphin pick-me-up is needed in those days where anxiety might be taking up unwanted space in your mind.

I want to tell you about all the things I do to take care of myself and I want you to think about the things you can do for you. It's important to give back to yourself: life is too short, babes, and you really do need to give yourself time to recharge if you want to put the most into everything you do.

> **'I believe self-care and body positivity are linked.'**

If we start by looking into each of the five senses, we can use these to help us find ways to centre ourselves. I try to add the following practices to my life when I can and I hope there might be something that resonates with you and your lifestyle here.

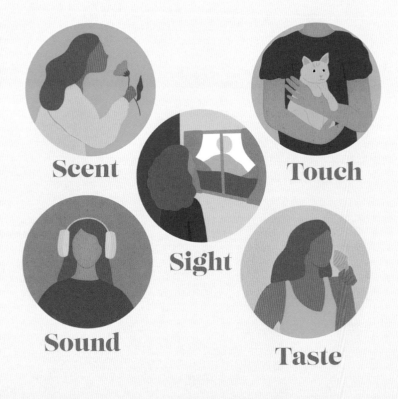

Scent

Touch

Sight

Sound

Taste

Sound

Meditation

It's so important to take time for yourself to just breathe. The world is such a busy place and often our lives become so stressful that the only time we really stop is when we sleep.

Meditation is something I used to think was for one type of person. The type who went to Thailand to go 'find themselves' on their parents' money during their gap year. But it really is an ancient universal practice that you can do anywhere, without special equipment or membership, making it accessible to all. It helps us slow down, even if we do it for just 15 minutes, and lets our minds rest properly.

> **'The world is such a busy place.'**

There are so many benefits to meditation that can make such a huge impact on our lives. Even a short period of meditation can give you the benefits of:

- **Reducing stress**
- **Promoting happiness**
- **Enhancing self-awareness**
- **Improving sleep**

These are all things that can greatly help us improve how we feel about our bodies. If you would like to try meditation for your self-care, here is a simple guide for beginners.

How to meditate

1. Find a quiet place to sit or lie comfortably.
2. Close your eyes.
3. Breathe naturally.
4. Focus your attention on the breath and on how the body moves with each inhalation and exhalation.
5. If your mind wanders, return your focus back to your breath.
6. Try to maintain this for 2–3 minutes if you're a beginner and increase the time limit each time you meditate.

There are also many different types of meditation practices you can explore. I personally like to listen to guided meditations with sound as they bring me extra relaxation. These can be found freely online and on many social media profiles of wellness practitioners.

Sound baths

This is an extension of a meditation
and something that has completely changed my life.

Practitioners claim that a sound bath can also work its magic
with anxiety, insomnia, stress relief and depression, all of which
are factors in our lives when we are dealing with negative
thoughts around our body image. The sound waves counter this
by gently coaxing your mind and energy into a state of
relaxation and peace.

What is a sound bath?

A meditative sound practice using soothing sounds created by
instruments such as Tibetan singing bowls, gongs, tuning forks,
chimes and various kinds of percussion.

How does it feel?

It will feel different for every person depending on the levels of
stress you have to release in your body. For me it feels like I
have been lifted into a cloud of sound, floating on the waves,
and I find it really opens my mind into a relaxed state.

How do you feel afterwards?
Absolutely zen, calm and at peace. You are told to drink plenty of water afterwards and then rest. I usually go straight to sleep once I am home.

Where can you do it?
There are so many sound bath studios you are bound to have one nearby (they are often connected to, or operate within, yoga centres), but there are also thousands of virtual classes you can join anywhere in the world, which are great to get a taster before joining an in-person experience (and you can always transport yourself to a different country or time zone, to make it feel even more of an escape).

My first sound bath

The Integratron in the Mojave Desert, California, is where I had my first-ever sound bath and will remain one of the most special memories in my life. Rising out of the desert in the middle of nowhere, this white dome structure has some very interesting history. It was built in the 1950s by ufologist George Van Tassel, who claimed the building was capable of rejuvenation, anti-gravity and time travel. Regardless of what you believe, the acoustics of this beautiful structure created the most incredible sound journey.

Playlists

Throughout the global pandemic of 2020–21, my mental health wasn't at its best. Like so many others, my life got completely turned upside down. I was used to being so busy, travelling and being around people, and suddenly I was alone for months. During this time, music therapy became a big part in my life. I created playlists for different days, different times, different themes and different moods so I never truly felt alone. Music is such a simple way to create instant joy and nostalgia.

I'm going to share with you the playlists I made and the top three songs in each.

Self-love: good morning

Big, fun, energetic tunes to awaken the mind and start the day with a smile.

1. **Curtis Mayfield – 'Move On Up'**
2. **Diana Ross – 'Ain't No Mountain High Enough'**
3. **Roger Sanchez – 'Another Chance'**

Self-love: cleaning

High-energy songs to get me in the mood to tidy.

1. **Tom Zanetti – 'You Want Me'**
2. **Quincy Jones – 'Soul Bossa Nova'**
3. **Groove Armada – 'I See You Baby'**

Self-love: bathtime

Fun and sexy songs to sing very loudly surrounded by candles and the drink of your choice.

1. **Barry White – 'Never Never Gonna Give You Up'**
2. **Rod Stewart – 'I Don't Want to Talk About It'**
3. **Hot Chocolate – 'You Sexy Thing'**

'Music is such a simple way to create instant joy and nostalgia.'

Self-love: calm
Mellow and peaceful songs to help you unwind before bedtime.
1. B-Tribe – 'The Sun'
2. Celeste – 'Father's Son'
3. Peter Gabriel – 'Heroes'

Self-love: disco
Songs that make you instantly wiggle that booty and put on a fabulous outfit.
1. McFadden & Whitehead – 'Ain't No Stopping Us Now'
2. Donna Summer – 'Could It Be Magic'
3. Tavares – 'Heaven Must Be Missing an Angel'

I also made these playlists collaboratively so friends, family and other people I connected with online could not only listen, but also add their favourite songs to the lists, too. Together we created a global playlist we can all enjoy and be a part of.

If you had to pick five songs under the playlist titles below, what would be your favourite and how do they make you feel?

Self-love: good morning

Self-love: cleaning

Self-love: bathtime

Self-love: calm

Self-love: disco

Touch

Crystal healing

Crystals have been a big part of my life for the last five years now. I wasn't open to them at first; in fact I remember my friend in New York would hide tumbles (small, rounded, polished stones) under her pillow and I would always laugh at her when we had sleepovers and say, 'Why are there rocks by my head?'

Fast forward to now and my collection is currently at more than 400 crystals in my house alone. And that doesn't include the little tumbles I now wear in my bra when I'm off to a work meeting and need a little extra energy boost, so that the bra isn't the only thing giving me support that day!

It all happened after I moved back from New York to London. I wasn't in a good headspace, I had no idea in which direction my career was going and to put it bluntly I wanted to try anything out that would give me some clarity, no matter if I believed in it at the beginning or not.

I bought some tumble stones from a crystal shop in Covent Garden in central London. The shop assistant told me to pick what I was drawn to, not what she would recommend, so I chose tiger's eye, carnelian, citrine and black tourmaline. I only found out the meaning of the stones after I'd chosen them.

Tiger's eye

This beautiful golden-brown stone is said to help with prosperity and motivation. It magnifies your confidence and pushes away any self-doubt.

Carnelian

This glowing orange stone is full of vitality and transfers courage and physical power to its wearer. It is also linked to passion, love and desire.

Citrine

Citrine helps to dispel negative traits such as fear and encourages optimism and clarity. It is also said to be a stone of good fortune and abundance.

Black tourmaline

This is popularly seen as a protective and grounding stone. It's used a lot in meditation and is also great at helping remove toxic energy from others who may be trying to drain your energy.

It seemed I had picked the ones I really needed at that time but I still didn't really believe they were going to do anything. I took them home and, as instructed, washed them under cold water and charged them under the light of the moon on my windowsill.

I woke up the next day and I booked three jobs. Now I didn't know if this was a placebo, or it had something to do with the idea of manifestation or maybe it was just a pure coincidence but whatever it was, my obsession then grew. In times where I felt sadness or a dip in my mental health, these little bundles of rocks in all their splendid colourings did bring me peace and my love for them increased. I would pick up crystals wherever I travelled, trying to source the native stones from where they had been mined.

> ## 'We are all connected to the earth and to each other.'

When you think about it, crystals are in fact little balls of energy that have formed under the earth's crust through extreme temperature changes. They are little scientific wonders, and they are full of natural energy that radiates from them, so it makes sense that we can harness some of that energy for ourselves. We are all essentially made up of chemical elements, the building blocks of life, so we are all connected to the earth and to each other.

Here are some of my favourites, which I would recommend for some self-care:

Rose quartz
This crystal is for self-love, self-esteem and confidence. It also helps you to feel compassionate towards yourself and others.

Amethyst
Opens up your intuition, connects you to your spiritual side and is a great protection stone for those struggling with anxiety.

Fluorite
Aids in concentration and promotes the flow of focus and calm (it has essentially helped me write this book).

Lepidolite

Helps to turn up your dopamine levels and release those feel-good chemicals hiding inside. It's also used to soothe anyone who has extreme mood swings.

Smoky quartz

Used for healing, grounding and letting go. It's a great stone to aid people carrying a lot of emotional baggage.

Clear quartz

This is one of the most versatile crystals. It's also known as the master healer as it can be used to amplify the energy of other stones. It purifies your energy and helps to release negativity.

Rhodonite

Heals the heart and emotional wounds from the past. It's a stone of compassion and an emotional balancer.

Sight

Gratitude diary

I have this book in which I write down one good thing that has happened to me every day. No matter how big or small, how funny or how serious, it gets written down.

Some days it might be: 'I achieved this project for work'; other days the highlight was a great grilled cheese sandwich I had made for lunch; or it could be that I laughed on the phone with my nan for an hour about how she's been stealing Grandad's whiskey from the cupboard and filling it up with water so he doesn't notice. It's little snapshots of my thoughts that brought me joy in that moment.

The book I have is actually a five-year diary. Each page has space to write for that specific day, but it covers five whole years. So once you have completed 365 days of journalling, you can go back and write under the same day from the year before. You will laugh, cry and feel the emotion of what you wrote a year earlier and I feel it has helped me with my overall levels of positivity – I find that I look back at the things that bring me joy and it makes me want to do more of them.

What is one thing you have done today that made you smile, no matter how big or small?

Full moon/new moon manifestations

I absolutely believe in the power of manifestation (see pages 111–13) and harnessing the power of the moon cycle is an important way to put these ideas out there into the universe.

Full moon

The full moon is a time to give yourself the power to let go. To do this, I write down everything that is no longer serving me – e.g. a toxic relationship, bad habit or worry. For example:

I cleanse myself from ...

This no longer serves me ...

I forgive myself for ...

I then burn the paper in a bowl and allow that energy to be released. If you have any crystals, this is also the perfect time to put them under the full moonlight to charge.

Regardless of whether you believe in this full moon ritual, physically writing down the things that are disrupting your life is itself a form of self-care. Acknowledging these things is an important first step in letting them go. Sometimes this is the hardest part.

New moon

Two weeks after the full moon is the new moon; this is the time you write down your intentions and manifest what you want to enter your life.

The new moon invites us to focus on new beginnings. For example, it might be a new career path, a new relationship or friendship, a better sleeping pattern etc.

Again, to do this I write down what I want to bring into my life. I then keep these hopes and dreams close to me to reflect back on in the future. For example:

I am ready to ...

I want to ...

I will ...

Scent

Essential oils

Aromatherapy and essential oils play a big part in my self-care.

Scent has been used for centuries to aid medicine, beauty and wellness.

I used to buy lots of mixes from high-end apothecaries but learned quickly that it is just as easy to make your own at home. I find the process of mixing my own oils quite therapeutic and it is so easy to do.

My favourite combination is called thieves' oil and is a mix of cinnamon, clove, lemon, eucalyptus and rosemary.

There is a tale that this mix was used by robbers during the bubonic plague years of the 14th century, when it was believed that this blend of essential oils created a barrier from the airborne disease to protect them while they went on the hunt. Whether this story is true or not, the combination of these scents is incredible.

To make this you will need to buy all the oils listed below and then mix a blend in another bottle – dark glass bottles are recommended. I would go for a 50ml (2fl oz) size to store this mix in. Here's the recipe:

- 40 drops clove bud essential oil
- 35 drops lemon essential oil
- 20 drops cinnamon bark essential oil
- 15 drops eucalyptus essential oil
- 10 drops rosemary essential oil

Now you have your thieves' oil blend you can do one of the following.

1. Add 10–15 drops to a water-based diffuser to fill your home with the aroma.
2. Add 10–15 drops into a similar dark glass spray bottle filled with water and now you have your own scented pillow spray.
3. Add 10–15 drops into a dark glass roller bottle with a carrier oil such as almond, olive or rapeseed, to create your own oil perfume roll-on.

I like to double the use of my pillow spray by storing it in the fridge to also become a refreshing face mist when a pick-me-up is needed.

Aside from the thieves' oil blend, my other favourite is lavender and geranium, to which I also like to add a fresh sprig of lavender to the bottle.

Here are some other essential oils that you could add to your self-care routine:

- **Chamomile** – aids in sleep, reduces anxiety and brings a calmness into the room.
- **Rose** – helps with soothing emotions, headaches and balancing hormones. Rose is known for strengthening the heart in periods of high stress, grief and depression.
- **Lavender** – calms the nerves, eases restlessness and improves sleep quality.
- **Geranium** – is a great harmonizer and can be used at the beginning of a hectic day or as an emotional restorative in the afternoon.
- **Fennel** – helps bring focus and clarity to wayward thoughts, and can be useful during times of doubt.

Important note: If you are going to try making any of the essential oil sprays please remember to check that you are not allergic to any of the oils.

Taste

Graze boards

Preparing a delicious meal takes time and sometimes we don't have a lot of it after a busy day. One thing I have taken joy in is curating graze boards inspired by such companies as Grape & Fig and Olive & Pickle.

I say curating, but they are literally so easy to do. Just grab a chopping board, a sharp knife and get out all the little leftovers and bits you've had in the fridge, plus the fruit that's been sitting in the fruit bowl all week and any nuts that have been in the cupboard for months.

Cut up the fruit and start placing it around the edge of the board like a little border, then start piling everything else in little bundles across the board.

Ten minutes later and *voila!*, you have made your own tasty little grazing platter from things that were left over in the fridge. Not only does it look cute, but you have reduced your food waste. You have essentially created an adult's buffet picnic, but made it chic!

How to fit self-care into your life

Those are my eight exercises I do in order to take some time for myself. Sometimes I do one of these once a week, sometimes I end up doing three in one day; how often you choose to do them depends on what time you have in your busy schedule.

It can be as simple as sticking on the self-love calming playlist while walking around the supermarket because it's been a long day, the queue is massive and you can't get the ingredients for your favourite dinner. It might be you've had a meeting cancelled, but that then frees up 15 minutes to try that new meditation app you've found. I'm aware we don't all have the time or resources to book a sound bath experience or go shopping for crystals all the time, but it's about finding joy in the snippets of free time you might find in your day and making sure you are taking that time out solely for you, no matter how long you have.

> **'It's about finding joy in the snippets of free time.'**

As I've mentioned before, self-love and self-care are subjective. You might think some of the ideas I've suggested are rubbish and they don't correlate with you. Or you might take the leap, try one of them out and suddenly find yourself with a new hobby or interest, joining Facebook geology groups to talk to hundreds of other crystal collectors around the world about who has the most interesting dream amethyst piece (I am guilty of this). Either way, the point I am making is that I hope there might be one thing from this chapter that you can try out for yourself and will bring you a little bit of happiness.

You are important, take that time for you.

Love Yourself

Don't wait until it's too late!

One thing I often think about is that, when you see older couples on holiday, they always seem to be happy and at peace with their bodies.

Lounging in the sun on white plastic deckchairs on the beach, the men wearing some snazzy multi-coloured peaked cap they've worn on every holiday since the 1980s, the women wearing a fabulous set of shades with a cute sarong and knitted tote bag featuring their favourite animal, while sipping on a piña colada and enjoying that sweet summer sunshine … they don't seem to have a care in the world, or be worried that their swimmers are probably a little worn and to the outside world maybe a little too 'small' for their figures at their age. (When

> 'Loving yourself can be the most powerful tool you can use, but the journey is a process.'

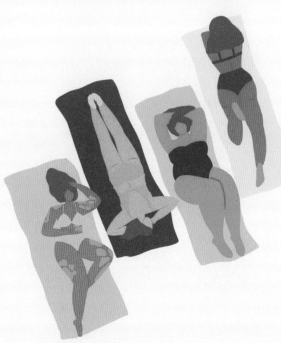

really, of course, you can and should be able to wear whatever you want, no matter what birthdate is on your passport.)

Clearly some people haven't reached that mindset yet. I recently got called out online by another plus-size woman, for posting an image of myself wearing a small bikini on holiday. She told me I should 'put it away' and wear something 'more flattering and classic like a 1950s' style', alongside some other verbal abuse.

To me, this woman is trapped in a body image trend of the past. She might believe that the 1950s was the only time her figure would have been appreciated; she might even believe in the toxic body shapes the fashion industry has created for us women (the apple, the pear, the hourglass, the upside-down triangle, to name a few) … but I don't. It's hard to be frustrated with someone who is quite clearly dealing with her own insecurities about her body.

If I were a UK size 8 (US size 4) wearing this bikini it would have been fine, but apparently a UK size 20 (US size 16) should not. Well, honey, I'm afraid we've moved on since then and now is our time to be accepted.

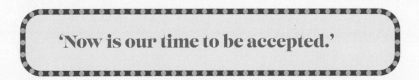

'Now is our time to be accepted.'

If we look at the older generation – I'm saying the ones currently in their seventies – we can see them lying on the beach without a care in the world. They have accepted their bodies for what they are and the journeys they have taken them on, and they are grateful.

These are the people who have lived from the era of the swinging sixties when Twiggy was the poster girl, through the eighties when the Special K/SlimFast diet ads were everywhere alongside the rise of the supermodel, to the time we currently live in. And now, in their later years, they've joyfully cast off all societal expectations.

The reason I am writing this is because I don't want you to look at the older generation finally finding their confidence in their mature years and feel you have to wait until you get to that age to experience this freedom and lack of restriction, too. I want you to have that mindset from when you're young, or to rediscover it *now*. I want you to free yourself from the false belief that a particular style of clothes can only work for one type of body.

What we're up against

I understand it's hard. We have so many popular shows on TV with little to no size diversity among the cast. The problem is that even the most desired celebrities and influential role models are under constant scrutiny to sustain the shape of their bodies. It's relentlessly stressful to live under the spotlight of social media and the online world. When even the most envied and successful people are suffering, do you see the problem with this picture? No one wins.

The truth is you don't need to aspire to be like anyone else when the best person you can ever be is yourself. The only way we are ever going to get there is by representation, especially in pop culture, in television and in the media.

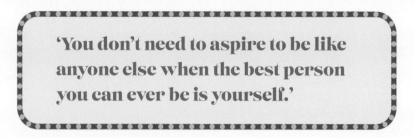

'You don't need to aspire to be like anyone else when the best person you can ever be is yourself.'

Bikini body bullsh*t

These TV shows with one type of body ideal make us believe that we need to achieve a BIKINI BODY READY aesthetic, which essentially boils down to: lose weight, tone up and aspire to look like a cookie-cutter version of everyone else. I want to tell you there is no such thing as being bikini body ready. You were always ready. You have a body; you have swimwear; there is a beach: *voila!* You are good to go.

Imagine if we said you needed to be SUPERMARKET READY. Special dress code, special body shape, weight and height to go get your weekly shop. It wouldn't happen, babes, so why are we letting people dictate whether we are ready to go and enjoy ourselves at the beach?

Can you see now how this is just a ridiculous marketing tool used to make you feel like you need to make changes in order for someone else to feed their company's bank balance?

Resist it!

The colour co-ord challenge

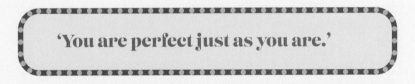

'You are perfect just as you are.'

Now I'm going to set you a challenge as I want you to try to really *feel* the statement above.

I've suggested doing this when you next go on a beach trip, but this idea can be tailored to your surroundings. If the beach is not an option, you could do this for a night out, a dinner or a sleepover.

Here's how it works:

1. Find a group of friends or family members you feel comfortable around.
2. Pick a colour that you all love.
3. All find beachwear/clothing of that same colour.

4. Turn up to the beach with everyone wearing the same colour (but different outfits).
5. See how powerful you will feel as your own little swimsuit biker gang.
6. Take a group selfie to remember the day.

I did this with a group of friends who were feeling down about their bodies and the changes they had gone through recently. I think a lot of us feel this way from time to time and this is a great way to counteract those negative emotions. If you have the chance to experience this with a group of your best pals, I would highly recommend doing it.

We picked the colour red. To me red is powerful, sexy and strong. I'll admit it was a challenge for everyone to find red beachwear. Looking for decent swimwear when you have more curves than a race track can be hard. But dressing in the same colour creates the same vibe, the same strength. It forges a unity. We made jokes that we looked like the new, modern-day version of *Baywatch* and renamed the group chat 'Slaywatch'.

The one thing I always remember about being younger was never being able to find the same items as my friends in clothing stores and always being the odd one out at sleepovers because my size was either sold out or not catered for. This day out took me right back to that moment and made me feel empowered that now, with my friends, we were a force to be reckoned with. Despite our differences, we were clearly a team.

Sometimes, when you have insecurities, they are the only thing you can focus on, but when you are enjoying life and being supported by others, a sense of empowerment can blossom.

> **'I feel happy about my identity, my body and my place in the world.'**

It's all about trying to find that sense of 'I feel happy about my identity, my body and my place in the world'. The aim is to forget about the part of you that you deem to be inadequate and instead work on building a strong, outward-looking mindset that overrides those inward-looking negative thoughts.

When you see that best friend of yours who has always hidden their arms, that friend who doesn't like to show off their legs because they are worrying about their cellulite (P.S. 90 per cent of women have cellulite by the way and it's experienced by women of ALL sizes) – when you see them throw off that cover-up and run into the sea because you are all there as a collective – it is honestly just so beautiful. We should be living this life free of cares and worries; life throws so much crap at us at times, we deserve some fun.

The power of you

As women, we go through a lot of changes in our lifetime, from puberty to menopause. Our bodies change, we menstruate, we might decide to use birth control (which in itself can change our bodies, our emotions and our libidos), we might decide to give birth, our bodies then stretch and grow to bring life into this world and after all of that we then go through menopause – and that only scratches the surface of what else might be thrown at us. This whole time we are being told how to look, how much to weigh, what to wear, how to behave and how to change.

Imagine the power we would have if we were truly, solely 100 per cent ourselves. Imagine how the world would be. We could teach society that diversity is, and should be, the status quo, that beauty comes in all forms and there would be full representation in all spaces. It would be normal to be diverse, not a gimmick for another campaign.

The only way to work towards this is by understanding and utilizing your personal power. Understanding that if you don't engage, follow, share or like any content you see online that doesn't fit into the narrative of what you believe to be honest, true and positive, people who practise body shaming won't be able to thrive in the same way. People who sell 'weight-loss' teas, advocate fad diets and, ultimately, perpetuate unrealistic body standards only do so because we support them. Even when we share them in private DMs to our friends saying how disappointed we are, we are still inadvertently boosting their brand. Once we get into the habit of not engaging with people who don't deserve it, the analytics, the engagement and the shares will go down and they won't have such sway over us. If you wouldn't accept this behaviour in real life, you shouldn't be doing so online, so blocking these people on the internet is your answer here. We can create a positive impact and rid ourselves of society's contrived image of what constitutes beauty if we erase the people who are contributing to this. Unfollow, unclick and delete social media accounts that don't bring you joy.

You deserve happiness. You deserve to feel that sun on your skin and not feel ashamed of your body. You should be proud your body has got you through the ups and downs of life and is still there holding you all together.

I know being on the beach, even with a big group of friends, can be daunting, but I want you to know that honestly, as much as it feels like everyone is staring at you, they usually aren't – they are just there trying to enjoy their holiday, too. Let's face it, the reality is that half of them will be four beers in, 20 minutes away from getting a dodgy burned tan line, and they're half asleep because they are happy they aren't at their desk in their 9–5pm job. The other half are busy worrying about their own body hang-ups that you don't even know about. They are trying to have that relaxation time as much as you are. So it's very unlikely they care what you or your mates are wearing.

Talking of relaxation, let's discuss how we can improve yours...

The love yourself list

I want you to write down the ten things that bring you happiness.

They could include a song that makes you smile, a person who makes you laugh, a meal that leaves you satisfied, a place that brings you comfort, a film that makes you wallow in joyful nostalgia, or an experience that you have never forgotten.

●●● *Love Yourself* ●●●

1.

2.

3.

4.

5.

6.

7.

8.

9.

10.

Now look again at the list. Which of these things have you done for yourself recently? I truly believe the key to loving yourself and improving your self-worth is by practising one thing a day that can bring you joy. Taking that time to have a moment purely just for yourself, no matter how big or small, can change the mood of your whole day. Self-love and self-care isn't selfish. Just like we need food for fuel, we need happiness and rest to recharge.

> '**We need happiness and rest to recharge.**'

I'm aware that life is busy; it's hard and it's fast. Most of the time I don't even manage to get through the basic routines of a day, but having this list of things pinned on a notice board, in the notes on your phone or written in a diary really does help when you need a little pick-me-up.

Remember though, this is all subjective to you. For some, self-love might look like a warm, soapy candlelit bath, while for others it's listening and dancing along to their favourite old records – you get where I am going here, right? No one can tell you exactly how to practise self-love; you need to explore the things that bring you joy personally.

You also may not be able to do those things all the time. You might be travelling for work, you might be dealing with trauma, you might have had no sleep, but remember: this list is your tree of self-care, the top ten things are the roots and each idea can have branches growing from it.

For example, one thing on your list might be listening to your favourite album from when you were a teenager, one that brings back memories of being with that special someone. Now you might not have time to dedicate an hour to listening to it this week, but let's say you made one song from that album your morning alarm sound. It's a small section of a memory that will wake you up and inject some nostalgia to kick-start your day. Sometimes it's not the actual task itself, but what you can branch out from it.

Final thoughts

I hope that reading this book has opened your eyes to society's toxic beauty standards. I hope you have been able to see how the majority of this pressure is simply a way for businesses to make money by preying on our insecurities. I hope that if you want to make changes to your body, you are doing it for you, not because you are comparing yourself to others, many of whom are lying about their appearance.

I hope you can see how incredibly beautiful you are when you are authentically yourself. I also hope that the questions I've asked you in this book will kick-start your positivity pilgrimage. Remember that you deserve this road trip of self-discovery, with the end goal being that you keep learning, discovering and evolving. Body positivity is all about self-love and that is never selfish: like they say in the onboard safety instructions on aircraft, you have to look after number one before you can help others around you. Find that inner confidence, help it grow and watch everyone around you, including yourself, benefit from this newfound energy you are bringing to the table.

'You deserve happiness.'

But there's one question I asked myself at the start of the book and I've been dying to answer it again now. So here goes: *does my butt look big in this?*

You know what, babes, yes it does. It's big, it's bouncy, it's covered in stretch marks and, let's be honest, it has so much personality it should have its own phone number. And all this is a positive thing. Not just because of today's trends, but because I have learned the power of representation, the power of not comparing myself to others and the journey to self-love. I am very proud of my growth, both in the derrière section, but also my whole body and mindset.

I've managed to tackle my own insecurities and grow into the woman my younger self would have been so proud of, and I can't wait for you to have this journey, too.

You don't have to look like a trend. You don't have to fit in. You just need to be 100 per cent, authentically you. Your bum can look however – big, small, wobbly, flat, dimply or bouncy – because it's yours and you are brilliant. You will be brilliant now, you will be brilliant tomorrow and you will be the same damn amazing person in your eighties reminiscing on your life, full of newfound admiration, kindness and strength for the best friend you'll ever have – your body.

You got this, babes. X